WORKING MEN'S COLLEGE.

LIBRARY REGULATIONS

The Library is open every week-day evening, from 6.30 to 10 o'clock, except on Saturdays. when it closes at 9.

This book may be kept for three weeks, If not returned within that period, the borrower will be liable to a fine of one penny per week.

If lost or damaged, borrower will be required to make good such loss or damage.

Only one book may be borrowed at a time.

SKETCHES IN
NINETEENTH CENTURY
BIOGRAPHY

" Thus they parted.   They are now in another, and a higher, state of existence ; and as they were both worthy Christian men, I trust they have met in happiness.   But I must observe, in justice to my friend's political principles, and my own, that they have met in a place where there is no room for Whiggism."

BOSWELL : " Journal of a Tour to the Hebrides."

SKETCHES IN

NINETEENTH CENTURY BIOGRAPHY

BY
KEITH FEILING

LONGMANS, GREEN AND CO
LONDON ✦ NEW YORK ✦ TORONTO
1930

LONGMANS, GREEN AND CO. Ltd.

39 PATERNOSTER ROW, LONDON, E.C.4
6 OLD COURT HOUSE STREET, CALCUTTA
53 NICOL ROAD, BOMBAY
36A MOUNT ROAD, MADRAS

LONGMANS, GREEN AND CO.

55 FIFTH AVENUE, NEW YORK
221 EAST 20TH STREET, CHICAGO
TREMONT TEMPLE, BOSTON
128-132 UNIVERSITY AVENUE, TORONTO

*Made in Great Britain
at the* BURLEIGH PRESS, *Lewin's Mead,* BRISTOL.

To
MY WIFE

CONTENTS

NOTE

The following studies, with one exception, appeared originally in *The Times* or the *Times Literary Supplement*. They are reprinted by kind permission.

PITT

PITT

IT is rather over 170 years since Pitt was born, but his historical era, if on its deathbed, is still faintly breathing. The problems which broke on him in torrents still flow round us, and the gulf of time between his age and ours narrows when we reflect that one member, at least, of the last Cabinet had seen the light before the woman whom Pitt once hoped to marry passed away. His lasting claims upon us in no sense belong to party. The words Whig and Tory never occur in his speeches; he used the faiths and formulas which they represent as means, not ends, and from the early grave to which party faction, hardly less than Austerlitz, consigned him, he seems to look round as if he, like Farinata, "holds Hell itself in deep disdain."

Upon the extraordinary career which began at twenty-four as Prime Minister, and ended thus at forty-seven, have long played searchlights of affection and malice, retrospective misapplication and false analogy; but nothing seems likely now to disturb his fame. Before 1914 it was open to any schoolboy to deride the fallacy of his Sinking Fund, to blame his conduct of war, to condemn the severity of his anti-pacifist legislation, but now, chastened by some comparative history, we incline to make more allowance; Pitt, at least, never despaired

—" I am not at all afraid for England," he told Burke; " we shall stand till the day of judgment."

He was, we must concede, a favourite of fortune, who presented him not only with his father's name, but with party opponents who made most inconceivable mistakes of tactics and exposed a deep lack of public character. The leader of the Opposition can, indeed, be largely excepted from this indictment, but all the charm of Fox, his uneconomic and impracticable generosity of ideal, cannot purge away the black faults of many who sat behind him.   For they—to say no more—degraded politics by making the Prince of Wales their lever, opposed war with an enemy who violated Belgium, would have offered up India on the party altar, and attempted to win by extra-Parliamentary pressure the position they persistently lost at elections or in reasoned debate.

To rest on your opponents' mistakes is not to rest on your laurels, and if Pitt's reputation depended on such negation it would long ago have perished; at best he would be remembered as one who, after breaking the Coalition, lived on in dumb contentment, self-crowned with the halo of saving society.   He did not live so; on the contrary, the founder of the new Tory party, who preferred to call himself " an independent Whig," lived the life of a ceaseless, radical reformer.   To demonstrate this we could, with justice, take only the years preceding the Great War, and refuse to judge, as it were from a punt on the Cherwell, the pilot who had to weather the storm.   Yet there are answers to be made to the stock indictment of Pitt as an apostate from

earlier ideals, and words of his own which make his retreat a Corunna.

One such word gives us, it may be thought, enough
defence for taking up arms against France : " What
we have gained by the war is, in one word, all that we
should have lost without it." And if war at all, he argued,
it must be won; consciously, therefore, and with repeated
candour on the demands of " security," he put aside
both his own reforming platform and the normal liberties
of civilian life. For this severity against anything that
might harbour defeat, he was called an enemy to the
Constitution. He threw back the charge; let it lie, he
said, at the door of those " who have exclaimed against
the injustice of bringing to trial persons who had associ-
ated to overawe the legislature; those who gravely and
vehemently asserted that it was a question of prudence,
rather than a question of morality, whether an act of the
legislature should be resisted; those who were anxious
to expose and aggravate every defect of the Constitution;
to reprobate every measure adopted for its preservation,
and to obstruct every proceeding of the executive government to ensure the success of the contest in which we
are engaged in common with our allies."

It could, again, be said that we should not judge Pitt,
as we are entitled to criticize the backslidings of a modern
Minister, who has in his hand a disciplined majority,
a party organization, and a party Press. From the
standpoint of constitutional monarchy, the reign of the
" good old King " constituted the bad old days, and what
the King, sane or insane, left over to possibility was
obstructed by the pompous political clans incarnate in

the Marquess of Buckingham. Even so, examination
in detail would suggest that no Minister but Pitt would
have moved Parliamentary reform in 1785, and that none
could have carried it after; that none but Pitt would have
fought so long against the Slave Trade, and that none
could have accomplished more for the Catholics than he
did. And if "apostasy" is in court, let the whole
chronicle be read; if in these well-known cases Pitt could
not convince his Cabinet and his party, let it be remembered that his largest project of social reform, for insur-
ance and family allowances, withered under the criticism
of Bentham and Burke.

More significant than these controversies is the temper
in which Pitt set about his work; work which is much
like ours. He found an Empire lately in disruption
and in course of change, old markets lost and established
industries dying, an outworn commercial system, new
and aggressive classes of society, party ties in dire
confusion. With all his faults and despite all his
problems, he left this project of modern England safely
in the way to something new and better, and what he
did in seventeen years is written large round us now.
He introduced eighteen Budgets, and in most of them
some sweeping innovation. To him we owe the very
scaffolding of national finance—the Sinking Fund and
debt administration, the first real audit, and the Con-
solidated Fund, the income-tax, the legacy duty, and the
principle of graduation. He inherited a tariff fast
bound in monopoly and prohibition, choked with
contradiction and wasteful vexation; by reduction and
simplification, preference and reciprocity, he welded the

instrument which Huskisson and Peel used in a world transformed. He began the process of relaxing the Navigation Acts and settlement laws; he launched the departmental reforms, in the Excise, the War Office and the Civil List, which Whigs and Peelites developed. He almost re-created the Navy. He remodelled the entire government of India. A treaty with the United States liquidated the War of Independence; another, with Spain, saved for the future the Canadian Pacific seaboard; in Eastern Canada he planted the germ of responsible government. He enfranchised the Irish Catholics, founded Maynooth, and legalized English Catholic schools.

In that vein of his action which some have deemed sentimental, he conceded the principle of outdoor relief to the poor and legal recognition to friendly societies. He would have abolished the " degrading condition " that the applicant for relief should lack all means of support; he advocated compulsory arbitration in industrial disputes; he appointed the London stipendiary magistrates. Beyond and overarching such construction in detail, his whole period of power was reform in action; his Regency Act finally put Parliament above the Crown, in practice he appealed from Parliament to the electors, his additions to the Peerage submitted them to the Commons, and his fortitude made the office, potentially so mighty, of Prime Minister.

As the years go on his speeches (if reported rightly) grow more frozen, he gets to be a man living for a single task, and we feel the life being ground out of the young Pitt of Wilberforce's friendship, who had blackened schoolboys' faces and treated Ministers like schoolboys, who "spouted" Waller or Lucan and was the soul of his society. But the essential character does not change, and, first and last, three great qualities seem carved in the personality and mind of Pitt—which is moderating, experimental, but ruthless.

Adherence in "speculative questions," he told Canning, he did not require, and in the conditions of his day no Minister could do more to secure breadth in his Government. The special element of the old Coalition to which he objected was not Fox's side of it, but the "old Tory" system of North, and neither in 1786 nor nearly twenty years later was it mainly his fault that coalition with Fox collapsed. It was not his doing, but that of his friends, that reunion failed with Addington; while the arrangements of 1794, the offers made at various times to Cornwallis, Tierney, and Henry Petty, show that he would outstep conventional party lines to gain strength for government. He seems to have had an almost unerring faculty of diagnosing a weak spot— to reconcile Ireland, to weld law-abiding Catholics to the Constitution, or to distinguish the majestic services from the questionable method of Warren Hastings; without emotion, and in the spirit of equity, he seems to pick out of destruction what can be used, or made positive, and pass on.

Born to construct, he rarely refused to reconcile what was reconcilable, "neither do I much admire," he said, "the philosophy of that person who thinks he has completed a beautiful new fabric when he has only completed the destruction of an old one." With reform, he argued, you " disarm the Jacobins of their most dangerous engine of attack "; and thus the abolition of the slave trade would point the contrast " between the wild, spurious, and imaginary tenets of the Rights of Man and the genuine principles of practical justice and rational liberty."

Though so vital a mind, Pitt was by personal temperament conservative, filled with old-fashioned sensibility, and not above the habits of his class. Men last at his ear could divert or capture a tired brain, but the persons near his heart were those he long had known. He enjoyed a ride to hounds, shot partridges in the year 1799, took his duty as Warden of the Cinque Ports like a Tudor Warden of the Marches, built and planted, talked bad French, kept up his classics, overspent, and drank quite enough. He believed in country life, on that argument defending the Game Laws, and refused, on the like ground, to treat as " unearned" the incomes of the country gentry, who in his eyes made the " cement" of society; for that matter, he held that taxation had revenue as its proper object and should not be used as a weapon of social reform.

Not that he lived in the past—no man less so—but he disbelieved in the whole theory of revolution, and the violence of his language against the Jacobins entirely consists with the reformer of 1785. " Prudent and temperate" schemes, so run the sweeping speeches of that year, " separated from every ingredient of faction, and from vague and unlimited notions," " the experience of our Constitution," " the original principle of representation," a House based on no theory of mandate but

B

yet " in perfect sympathy with the mass of the people "
—from all this we could predict the later denunciation,
which shocks the critic on the hearth.

For Jacobinism revolted every fibre of his being.
Bent upon actual, verifiable improvement, he despised
" the vain and false philosophy of late sprung up, which
refers all things to theory, nothing to practice—which
rejects experience, which substitutes visionary hypothesis
for the solid test of experiment, and bewilders the human
mind in a maze of opinions when it should be employed
in directing to action." The loud pretensions of its
leaders did not appal him, or " the dark designs of a few,
making use of the name of the people." He never tired
of asking the Commons first to look on this picture, then
on that—first at the beatific vision of fraternity, and then
at the September massacres. A lover of union, he found
the essence of Jacobinism to consist in a " system of
dividing the orders of the community," and in representing property " as the easy prey of the indigent, the
idle, and the licentious." As he hated the teaching, so
he denied the fact; classes in England melted impercep-
tibly one into another, " the line of union " was nowhere
wholly broken, the middle class ran like a connecting rod
from top to bottom.

When the war brought high prices and misery with
it, the remedies which he put to Parliament—rate-aided
wages, bounties on import, training schools or family
allowances—were in advance of a generation whom he
himself had taught to look up to Adam Smith, and
whom Burke had taught to look down to the anarchy
under their feet. But he would not carry the exceptional

measures which, he admitted, necessity must impress upon *laisser faire* beyond the demonstrable need of the hour, or take two steps, which might prove steps backward, when one would do. With "affectionate gratitude" he recognised the common suffering, but he declared it not only (as impartial history at last is proving) to be exaggerated, but not entirely remediable by any Government. He was not satisfied that the economic clock could be regulated afresh by any stroke of the pen. "If it be unwise to be guided solely by speculative systems of political economy, surely it is something worse to draw theories of regulation from clamour and alarm. If we ought not to bend observation and experience to any theory, surely we ought much less to make just principles and tried courses yield to wild projects, struck out from temporary distress, the offspring not of argument but of fear, not of inquiry but of passion, not of cool reflection but of inflamed prejudice. No man, therefore, who duly considered the causes from which the prosperity of the country has arisen, who well understood the foundation on which it stood, could think for a moment that, to redress any supposed mischief which, in times of peculiar scarcity and distress, monopoly might be supposed to have occasioned, it would be right to strike at the freedom of trade, and the application of industry and capital. To do so would be to bring us back to something worse than the system that prevailed five hundred years ago."

If we were asked for one continuous example of this experimental statesmanship, we could not hesitate to name Ireland, whose position in the Empire Pitt found a public danger and her domestic division a public degradation. He began with commerce as a bond of union, but not with Union in its full meaning; denied that avenue, he opened up another in Catholic concession as a step to common parliamentary reform, and, when Union at last seemed to him inevitable, combined it with Emancipation and State aid for the priesthood.

" What a strange mist of peace and war seems to hang over the ocean," wrote Gibbon in 1790; " we can perceive nothing but secrecy and vigour; but these are excellent qualities to perceive in a Minister."   Excellent, we can agree, if the vigour be so plain as to make secrecy legitimate; and legitimate it was in the case of this Prime Minister, whose actions are marked with brain, elasticity, hope and vigour.   His departmental reform made a holocaust of reversions ; he enforced, politely but firmly, on Grenville the high standard of disinterestedness which he applied to his own salary, and broke promptly the corrupt alliance of former Governments with moneyed men.   Nothing made him " so bilious," he said once, as Cabinet reconstruction, but few so freely reconstructed; nor did he wait upon personal affection, or decent intervals, for the weeding out of inefficiency.   He removed his brother with the same determination, though with very different expression, that he employed in the case of Thurlow.   Against Addington, after long resistance to multifarious intrigue, he moved, when he did, with resolution and on public grounds; his circular of April 1804 demands " a system of more energy and decision," and declares outright that " while the Government remains in its present shape and under its present leader nothing efficient can be expected either to originate with them, or to be fairly adopted and effectually executed." His Budgets teem with modern suggestion and admitted experiment—a " de-rating " for merchandise, a shop tax, or a betting duty.

Armed with this drastic gift, he was attracted to, and attracted, youth and reality, as none but the vital can ; having what Bagehot took as " the first qualification of the highest administrator," that is, " thought for something which he need not think of, of something which is not the pressing difficulty of the hour." In his prime he well realized the ossification besetting a legislature which is both a club and a social caste, for " we may keep the Parliament," he wrote of Ireland, " but lose the people "; and he grasped the power of the Press. From this realism proceeded the fact noted by M. Halévy, that " innovators love the young, and Pitt was an innovator " ; that the world of business voted Pittite, and that the new industrialism of his day was Tory. When he had gone they drifted elsewhere and looked to others for a lead—as did the young men whose service he had won : Wellesley, Huskisson, or Canning.

To cut deep, but to avoid the life-bearing arteries, seems the prescription of his early policy. " Let us look our difficulties in the face," repeat the Budget speeches; " a comprehensive system, suited to the needs of our situation," " a permanent and tranquil scheme "—principle, system, a facing of actuality, such is the doctrine of his youth, and one not wholly lost in middle age. An observance of dates reminds us that after the Revolution broke out he supported Fox's Libel Act,

granted elected legislatures to the Canadas and the
electoral franchise to Irish Catholics, and suggests that
time, pressure, and disease, rather than disillusionment,
explain the slow progress of reform in the last ten years.
Like other Ministers, he was compelled, or allowed
himself, to become immersed in minor questions—in
London docks, or waste lands, for instance, in 1794—
when the first Coalition was breaking.

The sword, then, outwore the scabbard, and, whatever
we think of the cause in which it was drawn, few will
judge it to have been other than finest, true steel. We
shall remember that, if ill-fortune made Pitt the fore-
runner of Eldon and Liverpool, he was spiritual father to
Canning and Peel; sanguine and optimistic though he
was, even to extremes, confident that the mass of mankind
were good, a reconciler and a man of rational expedience,
all these moderating and reasonable virtues were driven by
heroic energy and masculine purpose. Words that he
used of the war are equally true of his method in peace.
" Moderation I should consider as that virtue best adapted
to the dawn of prosperity; there are other virtues of no less
importance which are to be acquired under a reverse of
fortune; there are the virtues of adversity endured and
adversity resisted, of adversity encountered and adversity
surmounted."

When Bishop Pretyman consulted Pitt on the matter
of a thanksgiving sermon for naval victory, he approved
the text " Except these abide in the ship, ye cannot be
saved," but went on to suggest the moral. " Your sermon would be to prove that God, who governs the world
by His providence, never interposes for the preservation

of men or nations without their own exertions." After
a little pause (reports the Bishop) he said, " I really
think that with that text it will be the best sermon ever
preached." Mrs. Pretyman deplored " the weight Mr.
Pitt gives, and is desirous of giving, to human exertion ";
but if a Prime Minister must, as she said of Pitt, be
" a better politician than a divine," the world still calls
out for this political theology.

LORD LIVERPOOL

LORD LIVERPOOL

ON the 17th February 1827 his servants found the Prime Minister unconscious and paralysed beside his breakfast table, clutching in one hand a letter from Canning. For physical death he had to wait through nearly two years' misery, but politically he, and much with him, was this day dissolved ; this was the " one morning " we read of in " Coningsby," when " the Arch-Mediocrity himself died." A bitter feud, by him alone long restrained, now finally estranged Tories of the Right from Tory moderates, and within three years shattered the party which for fifty years had ruled the State and in nearly thirty years of war saved Europe. In 1832 aristocratic England of the four Georges disappeared : when the waters subsided, only a plank or two in Peel's new ship Conservatism reminded the world of the original Tory ark.

Robert Jenkinson, second Earl of Liverpool, had been given minor office by Pitt and in 1801, when just thirty-one, became Foreign Secretary ; from that date, one year excepted, he sat continuously in every Cabinet for twenty-six years. For fifteen of these he was Prime Minister : he was first offered it at thirty-six, he accepted it at forty-two. He fought, without appreciable loss, four general elections. His ministry included six of his successors—Canning, Goderich, Wellington, Peel, Aberdeen, and Palmerston—besides Castlereagh, Marquess Wellesley, Eldon, and Huskisson.

But within three months of his stroke the diarists speak of him as forgotten, and forgotten he remains. Part of this oblivion may be put down to his official biography, which is not a book, but a mausoleum. " Any drayman," Liverpool himself said, could have written Tomline's biography of Pitt; to read his own calls for more than physical endurance. Yet it is a bold assumption to hold that a politician gets the biographer he deserves, and a good policy may make bad reading.

Neither personal nor inherited endowments smoothed " Jenky's " road to power. In manner he seems to have been consequential, his neck was reputed the longest in Europe, and a flickering eyelid was a godsend to the writer who rhymed " blinking son " with Jenkinson. His aspect in debate, we hear from Canning's circle, was " as if he had been on the rack three times and saw the wheel preparing for a fourth," and his portrait has, indeed, that look of lowering strain, almost of torture, not uncommon in a generation of public men who died in their prime, often by their own hands. His father was only the grandson of conventional Oxfordshire baronets—curious descendants of that Antony Jenkinson who first familiarized England with the politics of Moscow—and though, as Bute's secretary and manager of Treasury patronage for North, he launched his son on a tide of Court favour, that alone sufficed no longer; it could neither raise Moira, nor depress Canning.

A vast official experience—and Liverpool managed

successively every principal department; a fund of carefully garnered information, which can be bodily transferred to Hansard—these may constitute a claim for any
post except the highest, but explain neither the initial
recognition of Liverpool as next in the succession, nor
his long and uncontested tenure.   These must be
ascribed to his possession, in high degree and by common
consent, of four primary ministerial powers.   He was
the most candid, lucid, and businesslike of speakers;
to that the testimony of hostile contemporaries like
Holland and Brougham is more convincing than his
recorded speeches.   He had a stout heart.   In the worst
days he never despaired of beating Bonaparte, as he never
failed in support of Wellington.   He formed his ministry
in 1812 in the face of all the talents, and of the Prince
Regent.   He maintained it in resisting those on whose
influence he depended, not only the first gentleman in
Europe but the first families in England, and contested
claims to patronage, from the Grenvilles and the
Wellesleys, with a force that gives a scanty glow to his
frostbound correspondence.   Even now the moral of
his letter to a brother, whom he sent to France after
Napoleon's escape from Elba, is no bad tonic in hard
times.   " In God's name, however, keep up your
spirits, or otherwise you can be of no use.   I do not
mean that you should not see things as they really are,
but you should not suffer yourself to despair.   I never
knew those feelings entertained by anyone, that they did
not, however unknown to himself, tinge the language
of the person who imbibed them, and thereby produce
incalculable mischief."   Again, though a party man, he

was a peacemaker and a patriot. He loathed coalitions, and refused to serve under Wellesley; yet he advised the old King to send for Fox. He defended Addington when he thought Pitt attacked him unjustly, but at his house they were reconciled. To this he added a loyalty to colleagues never impugned. Inheriting a legacy of vendettas, for fifteen years he harnessed them to one service—the irritable genius of Canning, the despotic Wellesley, the insensate rectitude of the Home Secretary Sidmouth, and the righteous ambition of Peel.

Whatever the justice, in modern times, of placing the onus of failure upon one man in a Ministry, two facts, that exist no longer, make it doubly unjust in judging Ministers of a century ago. Two powers equalled, even transcended, the Cabinet—the Crown and the country gentry—and one at least was a power of darkness. A personal foreign policy emanated from Windsor, intrigues in Cabinet from the Cottage or the Pavilion; the dynastic scandal of Queen Caroline shook the Government, distracted between a Queen who would not go and a King who continued to sin; the liberal treatment which was to save infant parliaments in Europe had to begin at home with the chartered liberties of Lady Conyngham. As for the independent country members, their passionate rejection of the income-tax, their heated cries of " the land in danger," reduced the Cabinet to financial expedients which at heart they disapproved; it is significant of the constitution of that day, that this opposition was independent of party and that its success was not held to necessitate resignation.

The ship of State, ballasted thus unevenly, lay rolling

in the trough of the storm which had revolutionized international relations, money values, industry, and ideals; if, as Sydney Smith says, this was "an awful period for those who had the misfortune to entertain liberal opinions," it was quite as awful to be Lord Liverpool. A great war debt pressed on the finances ; cessation of war and the recovery of our trade rivals created a sudden mass of unemployment; a vicious banking and currency system kept prices high, but in violent fluctuation; an inevitable poverty was enhanced by unorganized doles; an antique scheme of wage assessment which had retained, from a localized older England, the aroma of a "fair wage," collapsed under the blows of an " orthodox " political economy and a gigantic new capitalism; old standards having fallen, combinations of wage-earners were forcibly attempting to erect something new; the existing fabric of government, central and local, neither represented nor was fitted to cope with this phenomenon of industrial democracy. Outside England, legitimism under its high priest Metternich and its new convert, the Tsar Alexander, was struggling with fresh conflagrations of revolution.

How early, and with what decision, Liverpool's government detached this country from the Holy Alliance has only lately been imparted to us in full by the historians of Castlereagh and Canning. In demolishing that travesty of England's " reactionary " *rôle*, which did so much hard duty for the Edinburgh Reviewers, Professor Webster and Mr. Temperley have shown the essential assistance given by Liverpool to both ministers, whether in securing fair treatment for France, in establishing recognition of the South American States, or keeping a fair field for liberal institutions in Spain and Portugal. One spray of their hardly-earned laurels may go, then, to the Prime Minister.

For the connected triumph over legitimism's best ally in England, the King, credit goes to Liverpool almost alone. It is clear from earlier language regarding the *émigrés*, that he followed Pitt rather than Burke in these matters; that, though imbued with a Tory's deference for the Crown, he steered his course by facts, not fictions. Nor was he a Romantic; the sight of George IV in tartan did not transport him. The convivial loyalty reported from Edinburgh and Dublin must fall coldly on the Minister who, meantime, was clearing up the morass of the Queen's trial, or the treacheries of the King's communication with foreign States. On the major issues of government he was adamant. He capped the fight for recognizing " the New World " by threatening resignation—a word hardly ever off his lips during a two years' struggle to force the inclusion of Canning in the Cabinet. In 1820-21 Sovereign and Minister were barely on speaking terms; while George inquired anxiously as to his Prime Minister's temper, Liverpool made very clear to his colleagues the view he took of their master, considered as a study in constitutional monarchy. If the " principle of exclusion " was never again applied to the Cabinet by the Sovereign, to Liverpool it is largely due.

Embarrassed by the Tory apprenticeship of their strongest leaders, a powerful school of nineteenth century historians found it convenient to divide the domestic policy of Liverpool's ministry at the year 1822. For here, they argued, was the Hegira of Peel and Canning, two erring but still veritable prophets ; behind lies a darkness unrelieved, haunted by the shades of Sidmouth and Castlereagh, the Corn Laws, Peterloo, and the Six Acts.

But such dogmatic compartments are neither true of Liverpool's intentions, since he made unexampled efforts to include Canning in 1812, nor upon the sequence of facts. The most influential "Liberals" of the ministry later were Canning and Robinson; they were brought into the Cabinet in 1816 and 1818 respectively. Huskisson, another, fully supported the Corn Law of 1815; Canning, and for that matter Wilberforce and Zachary Macaulay, the Six Acts. A long list of constructive measures preceded the chosen year. In 1812 Protestant dissenters were freed from the dregs of the " Clarendon " code. In 1814 a generous peace was signed with the United States; the Company's East India trade was thrown open; the bounties on exported wheat came to an end. In 1819 final steps were taken towards resumption of cash payments, and the first Factory Act applied to cotton mills; in 1820 came the first Truck Act; the same year Liverpool blessed the Merchants' petition, which gave the first wind to the sails of free trade. It is true that Cabinet changes of 1822 put men of the new school in high office; for Peel replaced Sidmouth, Robinson succeeded Sidmouth's man, Vansittart, at the Exchequer, and Huskisson, to Eldon's anger, was given the Board of Trade. But new circumstances—agricultural revival, recovery of foreign markets, disappearance of the Queen—

c

contributed as much as new men to drive on a reforming policy, the lines of which had already been drawn.

Even in debating the Corn Law of 1804 Liverpool had shown his acceptance of the principle of *laissez faire*. He made exceptions; whether for agriculture, as a national bulwark, or for factory children, as in no sense free agents. But, for a man almost devoid of general principle, to this he deferred as much as to any one thing, arguing without ceasing that government interference must *à priori* be harmful, or that governments cannot make markets, though they may rid them of obstruction. His hand was, then, behind Huskisson and his Vice-President at the Board of Trade, Wallace, in the legislation which between 1821 and 1825 opened the doors for freer trade. Timber duties were reduced, Navigation Acts nearly nibbled away, prohibitory duties brought down to a 30 per cent. level, Canadian wheat admitted at a 5s. duty, free trade established between Great Britain and Ireland; before his death Government had once in emergency opened the bonded wheat and decided the principle of a sliding scale. Peel's reforms of the police, capital punishment, and transportation, the Bank Acts of 1826, the beginnings of slave emancipation in Crown Colonies, if taken with the Budgets and foreign policy, are at least worthy of commemoration as a footnote to the sort of history transmitted by Shelley and Cobbett. The combination laws of 1824-25 guaranteed, for the first time in any country, freedom of collective bargaining; whether the Government's first thoughts, in giving entire exemption from the conspiracy law, or their second, setting up safeguards against multiple intimidation, were the wiser, may be left unresolved. So, too, the grant of three-quarters of a million to relief works, but a million to building of churches, may indicate, after all, not the order of respective importance attached to these objects, but the state of the Exchequer; each forms part of a legislative total, unexciting but not unuseful.

Corn Laws, Peterloo, and the Six Acts, upon all of which a majority of contemporaries sided with the Government, make to most modern eyes a case against them— black, inhuman, and indefensible. This mental gap between our age and theirs goes down to the bedrock of economics and philosophy, and engulfs men of a mentality far removed from politicians. On the Corn Laws it must here be enough to say that protection was, and long continued to be, the panacea of the whole political class, and that the Government were moving at least as fast as public opinion towards freedom of imports. As to their social policy, it must, for the moment, be conceded that they were not called upon to deal merely with merry peasants and innocuous idealists. Forty years before, the Gordon riots had devastated London; in 1820 the physical force school attempted, in the Cato-street conspiracy, to murder the whole Cabinet. Luddite risings, frame-breaking, and the early story of trade unions are punctuated by arson and murderous outrage, and the too frequent use of the military was due to the absence of civil police. The " Manchester massacre " itself was directly brought about by panic-stricken local authorities, confronted with a long-rehearsed meeting of nearly 100,000 partly drilled men :

the Ministry's guilt extends not to the method of repression, but to their approval of the fact. Of the
Six Acts passed in consequence two (against illegal military training and traversing of indictments) have passed
into our permanent law. One, enabling magistrates in
certain named localities to search for arms, was in force
for two years only; the fourth, aimed at " blasphemous
and seditious libels," became commonly a dead letter
as to its drastic penalties, though in principle it continues ; a fifth submitted the cheap pamphlet Press
to the duty already paid by newspapers; the last, and most
severe, against public meetings unauthorised by local
authorities, applied only to open-air assemblies, and was
dropped at the end of five years.

All this, and more, may be true; constituted authority
must be defended, and a Ministry which preserves the
national fabric throughout huge revolutions merits more
than obloquy or oblivion. But history cannot be denied,
and though much of Disraeli's is fiction, the essence of
his summing-up against Liverpool and his colleagues
remains the truth : " He was peremptory in little questions, and great ones he left open. . . . Like all weak
men, they had recourse to what they called strong
measures. They determined to put down the multitude.
They thought they were imitating Mr. Pitt, because
they mistook disorganization for sedition." The Prime
Minister's comments on these portentous events did indeed light up the decorous blind alley of his mind.
He disapproved the Manchester magistrates' action,
but conceived that authority must be shielded, right or
wrong. The lamentable turbulence of industrial cities

could only be increased by Parliamentary reform. Any repression was better than mob rule.

This unvarying neglect of spiritual causes, this exhausting immersion in external fact, was the teaching he had gathered from men and politics. An early letter discloses the guilt of his Christ Church tutor : " My tutor has frequently thought that I have been too much run away with by general ideas . . . this I endeavour to correct." Burke, whom he took for an " oracle," and Canning, whom from Oxford days he was always following and restoring to his pedestal—each further impressed upon Jenkinson, who for that matter saw with his own eyes the storming of the Bastille, his original dread of ideas. In this departmental mind the fashionable teaching of *laissez faire* found a receptive soil; action must be cautious, it is commonly harmful, things will find their level. And so a native germ of immunity from "high-brows" settled into a contagious and certifiable disease.

He showed all its symptoms in aggravated form; the lack of relativity and proportion, a preference for uncontroversial and fragmentary improvement to drastic schemes, an inability to discern, amid a swarm of problems, the one or two which are vital. They were not inconsistent with a liking for efficiency, a shrinking from harsh action, an incessant good will. " Much too pacific a minister for Ireland," wrote Peel when the Prime Minister opposed coercion; " it is recommended to wait and see," growled Sidmouth in 1819, when repressive legislation was delayed for inquiry. His mind was ever open, but rarely to the root of the question;

he was on the side of the angels, but like them refused
to tread; scapegoat of that political catastrophe, when
the first-class brains are not trusted and the second-class
brains cannot see, he sat in that intermediate Micawber-
like office, waiting for things to find their level.   As a
young man he had seen Burns's funeral and wondered
at the pother men were making; in his later days he
found Coleridge unintelligible; the disease went deeper,
one must believe, than Wellington's odd theory of too
much reading the *Quarterly*.

When men asked for cheap bread, he offered the
Caledonian Canal; when pressed for game laws and poor
laws, he could point with satisfaction to the emancipated
negro or the liberalized Portuguese.   To English
Catholics he was prepared personally to concede the
franchise, but not to repeal the Tests ; on Emancipation
as a whole he was waiting to be convinced that it would do
any " practical good."   He was willing to disfranchise
Grampound, or any demonstrably rotten borough, but
saw no force in arguments for a general measure.   One
of his last letters to Canning predicts " a storm on corn "
from the agriculturists in the Commons; not a hint that
his vision ranged beyond them.   His was the sound near-
sight of a man " good in Cabinet "; his common sense
could dispose of tangible things thrust upon it, he could
see full well that Canning, and not Wellington, must
succeed Castlereagh.   But of that second sight, conceded
to greatness, he was devoid; his vision seems dimmed by
despatches and trade returns, his hearing obstructed by
the clubs and departments.   The ' Thing ' that Cobbett
abhorred has captured him; he cannot realize the un-

represented energy of the North, or feel that humanity
sentenced to transportation for petty crime.

But justice is distributive under representative government, and we have ceased to demand greatness from those
who have greatness thrust upon them. The Judaic rule
of our older historians, that one man should die for the
people, must be relaxed in the new-found study of mass
opinion. This overworked Prime Minister has been
pilloried long enough for the faults of millowners and
justices; for severities in which he was overborne by
Eldon, for omissions which he shared with Peel. If
any new epitaph is to be carved on his tomb, it is like to
condemn, not the man, but the party that raised and
restrained him; the Tory passing by may reflect, that
within this narrow ground of intelligence and achievement
lies all the power for good conceded by his forerunners
to this Prime Minister, for fifteen years chosen leader
of a great Parliamentary majority, a man of good will.

CANNING

CANNING

IT becomes every day more apparent that the rather painful road trodden by our forefathers at the close of the last great war is the same we shall ourselves traverse for the next generation. The circumstances are different, we shall arrive at different solutions, but we shall be dealing with a parallel set of problems. We, too, shall have our Reform Bill, our Combination Laws, and our Poor Law; it is possible that from the reverse end we shall repeat the controversy of the Corn Laws or the Bank Charter. If this is so, no greater disaster could befall modern Conservatism than to take its inspiration from one-half only of the Tories of 1815-50, or to swing so far against the verdicts of the last century as to find ourselves defending causes that are in fact indefensible.

Such reflections are suggested by the prominence given of late to Castlereagh—a great Foreign Minister, it is now conceded, who worked on lines far broader and more generous than his early critics allowed, but a man who in domestic politics was unyielding and unimaginative, and represented only part (and that not the highest) of the whole Tory tradition. For there are two sides to the history of any great political party, as it takes two to make a duel. Instinctively one's eye turns to the other

35

figure in that duel, fought in the body and with leaden bullets in September, 1809, on Putney Heath, but spiritually ever since continued. It is good that historical justice has at last been done to Castlereagh, but if it were at the price of extinguishing the Canningite philosophy of politics, it would be a dear bargain. Nor is this possibility an idle fancy. The old guard of reactionary opinion never surrenders, and, since it expresses feelings common to us all at moments, dies only to undergo periodic resurrection. The general disillusion with the aspirations of the Victorians is showing its worse side in curious political atavisms. Parliamentary institutions in Europe have never been weaker since 1832, and even in this country there are those who would short-circuit democratic government. In some this takes the shape of a pathetic belief in a reformed and predominant House of Lords; others declaim the idyll of the referendum; a third group hope to import the Roman dictatorship and the Abyssinian terminology of Fascismo into the country of Pitt, Peel, and Gladstone.

It is high time, it is submitted, to turn to the other branch of the party of authority; to turn from the defenders of institutions to the creators of belief; to turn, since this is the dualism last presented to us, from Castlereagh to Canning. One initial advantage, at least, accompanies this choice, since Canning, unlike his rival, was an orator, and the exposition of ideas which the research of a century has barely accomplished for Castlereagh can be gleaned from a hundred speeches of Canning.

The see-saw in historical reputations, which proceeds

in more or less accord with the advance of knowledge, has in his case been particularly violent. The age subsequent to the first Reform Bill idolized the acutest opponent of Reform. Gladstone bore to him hereditary allegiance. Disraeli vindicated him, the better to destroy Sir Robert Peel. His liberal foreign policy was inherited by Palmerston, and it became the fashion of nineteenth century historians to contrast him with the "wooden" Castlereagh, the familiar of Metternich and the "author" of Peterloo. Catholic Emancipation and free trade seemed the logical legacy of the liberalizer, and were carried into law by Peel and Wellington, the very men who had abandoned him in his greatest need. The feeling now is all the other way. "The more I study the matter," said Lord Morley to Lord Balfour in 1891, "the more do I feel that time makes Castlereagh bigger and Canning less," and in this he heralded the opinion of our own day.

His most ardent apologists cannot class Canning with those great public characters who fire nations to heroic action or lift their country to a higher moral plane. His ablest contemporaries respected his talent, but nevertheless distrusted him radically. "The joker," "the merryman," "a mere fluent sophist," "a light, jesting, paragraph-making man," ambitious, treacherous, self-seeking —all this, and much more, we may find charged outright by Grey, Hazlitt, or Sydney Smith, and endorsed, with or without reluctance, by Peel, Wellington, or the brilliant Lady Bessborough. Those who most loved or admired him, Pitt or Byron, condemned that voracious ambition. His own personal following in politics can be counted on two hands, and Huskisson was the only man of the first rank among them.

The egoism which made this desert round him devastated his first political period. He plagued the dying Pitt with immoderate feuds and moderate verses. He intrigued successively against his colleagues in the Cabinet—Hawkesbury, Castlereagh, and Percival. His share in negotiations for office during 1804, 1812, or 1822 leave an unpleasant taste behind. The decency of his private life, the devotion of his few intimates, innumerable kind offices to younger men, make no adequate answer to these facts. We are dealing with a public man, not with a *paterfamilias*. But if private morals should not enhance, neither, it is submitted, should flaws of character be allowed entirely to obscure transcendant public merits in a politician. We do not take the lack of morals or *morale* in Marlborough, Fox, or Nelson to minimize their memorable services to their country, and a suspect private character need not detract from the value of lasting lessons bequeathed to a political party.

" His principles," said Brougham, " were throughout those of a liberal Tory "—a larger class, it may be noted, than the party organizers usually allow. Canning himself gave to this definition a personal connotation. " Since the death of Mr. Pitt, I achnowledge no leader; my political allegiance lies buried in his grave "; at the foot of which his body was, in fact, also buried. Pitt and Burke are the only authorities he deigned to recognize in his speeches.

But when he took these for his leaders, he took them

as they were when he himself entered politics—no longer
peacefully labouring at economic or administrative reform, but engaged in a fight to the death with the French
Revolution. " Jacobinism," wrote his friend Charles
Bagot, " *that* is the antagonist of Canning," and from this
enemy he was rarely to escape. Here, probably, lies the
peculiar relevance of Canning's career to our own problems; in the lessons he deduced from a struggle of twenty
years with principles which to him seemed to involve the
end of the stable England he admired. His political
teaching never, of course, approaches the dizzy mystic
heights along which Burke alone could walk in safety;
it does not even cut so deep as the more prosaic wisdom
of Pitt. His arguments rarely reach the upper air of
ideals. They were suited to his constituents at Liverpool,
they represent the strength of fact, of necessity, and of
nationality, of those everyday forces, in short, which
move average humanity. But they were arguments
carried to perfection by a practical genius.

His first and wholesome asset was that " he gloried in
the name of Briton." His denunciation of " French
principles," marked from his earliest correspondence,
came from patriotism as much as from philosophy.
He never saw reason to think that Britain required
political instruction from abroad, and his first deduction
from the great war was that patriotism is prior, and
superior, to internal reforms. " It is idle, it is mere
pedantry, to overlook the affections of nature. The
order of nature could not subsist among mankind if
there were not an instinctive patriotism; I do not say
unconnected with, but prior and paramount to, the

desire of political amelioration." He delighted that the war had tested this question; that we "should be authorized, by undoubted results, to revert to nature and to truth, and to disentangle the genuine feelings of the heart from the obstructions which a cold, presumptuous, generalizing philosophy had wound round them." True, he adds, " of late a chill philosophy has been busy " in numbing " the natural enthusiasm of a brave people " —in " rendering them dead to the glories of Waterloo, but tremblingly alive to the imperfections of Old Sarum. But it will not do." What he meant by Britain, as opposed to the cosmopolitan " humanity " he mocked at in the *Anti-Jacobin*, will appear later from his foreign policy. Here one need only recall his word to Bagot on returning to the Foreign Office in 1822 : " For Europe, I shall be desirous now and then to read England."

But the whole temper of Canning—so pragmatic, sinewy, and rational—went to produce this dislike of formulas and systems. He resented them, in the first instance, as restrictions on energy. " Away," he cried, " with the cant of ' measures, not men,' the idle supposition that it is the harness, and not the horses, that draw the chariot along." In times of peril, " when precedents and general rules of conduct fail," nations fall or rise " not by well-meant endeavours (laudable though they may be), but by commanding, overawing talents—by able men." He distrusted formulas, further, because he preferred to reason from facts. Judge the French, he suggested in 1798, not by their theories but by the fruits of them. Look at the sister-republics

immediately connected with France; consider the degree
of liberty allowed to the Cisalpine, " whom in preference
to the others she appears to have selected as a living
subject for her experiments in political anatomy; whom
she has delivered up tied and bound to a series of butcher-
ing, bungling, philosophical professors, to distort and
mangle and lop, and stretch its limbs into all sorts of
fantastical shapes and to hunt through its palpitating
frame the vital principle of republicanism." His was
not the last age which has seen this surgery at work:
the Alps could be amended, for example, to the
Caucasus.

Judge Great Britain, he repeats, by her victory.
" Here is a fabric constructed upon some principles not
common to others in its neighbourhood; principles which
enable it to stand erect while everything is prostrate
around it." What is to be thought of the carpers who
cry " we like not this suspicious peculiarity," and " in
the spirit of this perverse analysis " proceed to dissect
a Constitution which, he wrote in 1792, was " by much
the best practical government that the world has ever
seen " ? Just in the same way he argued thirty years
later that, if the House of Commons was " adequate to
the performance of these its legitimate functions, the mode
of its composition appears to me a consideration of secondary importance." Lastly, he protested all his life long
against political cant. Nowhere did he deem it more
dangerous than in the realm of foreign affairs; he demurred
to moral rectitude as the test of desirability in alliances,
and denounced the illusion that the peace of Europe is
best secured by private virtues. " I do not know, sir,

D

but an alliance with a Mahomedan may be as good as a peace with an atheist."

But Canning not merely resisted abstractions in general; he criticised the revolutionary formulas in particular. He opposed to them the social and historically-minded utilitarianism of Burke, and anticipated that view of our " territorial " constitution which Disraeli was to restate once for all. " Government," he thought, " is a matter not of will, but of reason," and depended on no scheme of individual natural rights. Neither Roman Catholic nor Dissenter had any claims, inherent in them as men, to any franchise or employment. Such claims in a civilized society were subject not only to limitations of circumstance, but " to lasting control from the necessity of the State." The ground of claim to office was, rather, " wealth, ability, knowledge, station," a variable, an elastic, but yet a real test. No word in politics, he held, was more abused than the " people," if it were applied, as commonly was the case, " to a portion of a community arrayed against the interests of the nation." To him " the people, as synonymous to a nation, meant a great community, congregated under a head, united in the same system of civil polity for mutual aid and mutual protection, respecting and maintaining various orders and ranks, and not only allowing the fair and just gradations of society, but absolutely built upon them." Revolution, and its " theories and preternatual purity," would break the ties thus connected by Providence. " Naked, abstract, political rights are to be set up against the authorities of nature and of reason." " Ancient habits, which the reformers would call prejudices; preconceived attachments, which they would call corruption," everything consecrated by time and usage, was to be cleared away before the *tabula rasa* of the New Jerusalem. This was not the spirit of the law of England, which was " eminently a spirit of corporation. Cities, parishes, townships, gilds, professions, trades and callings, form so many local and political sub-divisions, into which the people of England are distributed by the law; and the pervading principle of the whole is that of vicinage, or neighbourhood." To Canning, nature and nationality have arranged the order of society, and nature could not permanently be circumvented. The sequel will show that he was far from a blind acceptance of the principle of private property; for he was not one of those Tories who borrow the first article of their belief from Locke and the Whig philosophers. But he did, clearly enough, view property as " the conservative principle of society," and as something so inherent in man's nature that no amount of enfranchisements could destroy its political vitality.

Canning's predictions upon Parliamentary reform may seem to some to reveal the blind spot which somewhere will be found in the most ardent reformer. They depend in part on arguments easily appreciated by contemporaries of Bonaparte, but now unfashionable; as, for instance, that the certain end of extreme democracy is military despotism. Yet, as part of his mentality, they cannot be ignored, and have a certain cheerless accuracy all their own. He set out, of course, from the general principle, or rather denial of principle, that we have seen already. " I confess that, as in private life I generally look with caution on that diffusive benevolence which neglects the circle immediately round it, so I look with some little suspicion to that spirit of general improvement which is ready to sacrifice, to a general principle, the immediate and particular safety of its own country." He did not feel bound " to enter the lists to show why the British constitution should be a monarchy "; it was enough for him that many generations had made it so. Now to the reality of monarchy he attached a real importance, and much as he disliked "aristocratic combinations," he hated still more the plain uniformity of democracy. " All simple forms of government are bad." " A simple democracy is tyranny and anarchy combined." And if extension of the suffrage were given upon "principle," he did not see how one could hope " to control it in degree." The Crown, as a living force, would inevitably disappear; so must the Lords, for " by what assumption of right could three or four hundred great proprietors set themselves against the national will ? " so we should arrive at the portent he dreaded, a democracy " inlaid with a peerage and topped with a crown." He, then, could not subscribe to those hopes of " finality " with which the Whig leaders flattered their supporters.

Whatever may be thought of the logic or the value of such prediction, the sequel to the great war merely strengthened Canning in the convictions formed during the Revolutionary era. The menace, he wrote in 1818, was more serious than in 1793, and no one defended more strenuously than this liberal Tory the absolute necessity of the Six Acts. " We ask them not against, but for, the people—for the protection of that sound and sober majority of the nation, for that bulk and body of the community, which are truly and legitimately the people." It was folly to believe that "the monstrousness of any doctrine is a sufficient security against the attempt to reduce it into practice." Good-natured men in France had smiled in 1789 at the depth of the popular delusion, but since then French soil had been "deluged with the best blood of the nation." The contemporary Socialists, the Spenceans, might not permanently succeed in making the land national property, but "they would labour hard to accomplish the spoliation of its present possessors." Never dream, he concluded, that the small beginnings of sedition are contemptible, for "the sportive relaxation of rebellion is in blasphemy." It was their duty to guard the Constitution, and as regards imported doctrines he did not despair : "in the very worst of times there was inherent in the English constitution, or rather in the constitution of the English mind, that which would repel the aid of foreign treason."

So far we have Canning as the champion of established institutions and tried policy; it is time to consider him as their liberalizer. For here was the rent through which the envious Cascas stabbed. It was on account of his advocacy of Catholic emancipation that the University of Oxford refused to accept him as their burgess; it was his advanced foreign policy which called forth the intrigue of George IV and of Wellington.

At first glance the contradiction is glaring. The head of the opposition to Parliamentary reform is the protagonist for Catholic emancipation; the arch-enemy of revolutionary France is become the headstone of the corner against Metternich, and goes down to posterity as the friend of Greece or of Portugal, and the joint maker of South American independence. But the intellectual consistency is, in fact, perfect. His mind has, indeed, the qualities of the eloquence which expressed it—its masculine reasoning, its hatred of exaltation or abstraction, the faculty of eliminating all that is secondary to the necessity of the hour. But, if this was opportunism, it was opportunism swinging upon fixed and constant poles. The interest of Britain and the experience of Europe provided them. He never, it is true, believed in the coming of a millennium, when the British Navy might be trained " on the margins of duck-ponds and the towing-paths of canals." He thought that pacifism in the long run meant unnecessary bloodshed, and upbraided those who " would let aggressions ripen into full maturity, in order that they may then be mowed down with the scythe of a magnificent war." The doctrine of splendid isolation, with its " delusive mixture of whining despondency and false security," appeared to him a national heresy. " To be unpresuming is not necessarily to be safe," and he held that Britain, given her situation and her history, must be great in order to be happy. " The choice is not in our power . . . we must maintain ourselves what we are, or cease to have a political existence worth preserving."

But the greatness of Britain, in home as in foreign affairs, consisted in freedom from two dangers—foreign domination and revolutionary change. He applied the same criterion to Europe, and would resist any, whether a Metternich or a Bonaparte, who threatened one or the other. "Our business is to preserve, so far as may be, the peace of the world, and therewith the independence of the several nations which compose it." He would not, like some of his successors at the Foreign Office, restrict this principle of non-interference in favour only of "liberal" States; he would let it shine both on the just and the unjust. Like some later Conservatives, he judged present peace more valuable than distant perfections for the labouring mass of humanity, and evinced no objection to absolute monarchy—"where it is the growth of the soil, and where it contributes to the happiness or to the tranquillity (which, after all, is the happiness) of a people." But Metternich, he always argued, was the real firebrand of Europe, for he was doing his best to hasten on a struggle between the bare ideals of despotism and democracy. "The harmony of the political world is no more destroyed by the variety of civil institutions, in different States, than that of the physical world by the different magnitude of the bodies which constitute the system"; no more, indeed, in Canning's view, than the working of the British Constitution was impaired by the diversities of franchise in the unreformed Parliament.

The European settlement of 1815 rested, he ever repeated, upon a compromise between the rival principles of order and independence; but if Metternich's system brought them again into collision, "the most consistent anti-revolutionist may well hesitate," ran his warning of 1823, "which part to choose." As to the deciding element at any given moment in the public action of Britain, this Canning did not affect to conceal. "The grand object of my contemplation is the interest of England." Providentially, her station was "essentially neutral; neutral not only between contending nations, but between conflicting principles." In seeking her interest, which was the peace of the world, she must weigh the armed dangers on either side of her neutrality; "it is upon a just balance of conflicting duties, and of rival, but sometimes incompatible, advantages, that a Government must judge when to put forth its strength." For a minute one catches from Canning the echo of wise Venetian senators, looking out from their solid insularity on an Italy torn between mobs and tyrants.

We come, finally, to the liberalizer of Toryism. Good policy, within as without, consisted, he thought, in finding that golden mean between freedom and order which empowers ancient institutions to maximize national energy and happiness. Eight weeks before he died, in the house at Chiswick where Fox had died " a Briton," he gave his conclusion on the whole matter. " We are on the brink of a great struggle between property and population. Such a struggle is only to be averted by the mildest and most liberal legislation." The sting of his prophecy lay in its tail : " If the policy of the Newcastles and the Northumberlands is to prevail, that struggle cannot be staved off much longer." Eighteen months earlier than this he drew at full length his notion of domestic legislation. The Government, he said (the refusal to re-open the question of Bank restriction was the ground of attack), were charged with lapsing from the principles of Mr. Pitt. " It is singular," begins the famous reply, " to remark how ready some people are to admire in a great man the exception rather than the rule of his conduct. Such perverse worship is like the idolatry of barbarous nations, who can see the noonday splendour of the sun without emotion, but who, when he is in eclipse, come forward with hymns and cymbals to adore him." Only necessity had made Pitt swerve from his original ideals; " we must deal with the affairs of men on abstract principles, modified, however, of course, according to time and circumstances." Some persons, who would have persecuted Galileo or suppressed Turgot, "think that all advances towards improvement are retrogradations towards Jacobinism." But the duty of a British states-man was to keep the balance even—" not adopting revolutionary fantasies, but not rejecting, nevertheless, the application of sound and wholesome knowledge to practical affairs, and pressing, with sobriety and caution, into the service of his country any generous and liberal principles, whose excess, indeed, may be dangerous, but whose foundation is in truth. This, Sir, in my mind, is the true conduct of a British statesman, but they who resist indiscriminately all improvements as innovations may find themselves compelled at last to submit to innovations although they are not improvements."

In this spirit he approached the subject of Catholic emancipation. Expressly disclaiming any argument based upon inherent rights, he planted himself on the firmer ground of utility and fact. Exclusion was exceptional, and inimical to the British Constitution; citizens of the same State " are entitled *prima facie* to equal political rights and privileges." National unity must be admitted to be desirable in principle, and the *onus probandi* lay on those who obstructed it. When for several generations "a great permanent cause of political discontent" settles down upon part of the nation, it is the duty of any government to dispel it. Coercion was no remedy; "firmness and decision are often good things, but they become either virtues or vices, according to the uses in which they are employed." As for those who cry, "Follow the wisdom of our ancestors," Canning pertinently answered, "Which ancestors?"

He made the true point that the penal code, like all our institutions, had undergone development, and had never been a finished system ; far less was it so now, since the concessions of 1778 and 1793. May we never learn from our ancestors' mistakes, he asks ; may we never allow "for the different genius of different ages"? Extermination had been tried in Ireland and had failed. "We have adopted the principles of the more generous counsel ; shall we halt in the pursuit of it, or try it fairly to its end?" But while declaring the concession overdue, Canning refused to cast the power of Government behind the measure if it would cause convulsion in England ; "a single week of peace in England is worth a much larger portion of time devoted to the accomplishment of a great, but yet partly a theoretical, good in another portion of the Empire." It was on the same lines of empirical caution that he was proceeding, with Huskisson, to deal with the tariff, when death intervened.

No political future in our history is more tantalizing. Would the Liberals he had taken into his Cabinet have drawn him, like Gladstone later, definitely away from the Tories, or could he, like Disraeli, have educated his party ? His teaching may, at any rate, stand permanently on record as that of " a liberal Tory " at the close of the last great war.

A compound of Burke and Pitt, he showed (is it not nearly certain ?) how Pitt, had he lived to be sixty, would have dealt with the tail of the storm. He had at least one supreme merit of the teacher—that he had been a persistent learner. He had realized, from twenty-five killing years, upon what British policy rested : on the order and the freedom developed by the nation's history. He refused to sacrifice either. He would not plunge forward in obedience to abstract speculation ; he would not stand still at the dictation of foreign Powers, or of class prejudice. He believed in the reasonable public opinion of a great country. No view of his forbade him to accept improvement ; every principle bade him never agree to revolution or reaction. He believed in intelligence working old institutions. If he distrusted Parliamentary reform, he showed to posterity how much social progress may be advanced within the bounds of an ancient fabric. Mere sentiment or bare propositions offended his rational mind, which yet was much more deeply rooted than in the intellect alone, for he trusted to the whole experience of his country and the whole nature of man. He did not cant ; neither was he a cynic. Himself not disclaiming the title of " adventurer," with which he was loaded by his intellectual inferiors, he believed in a conservatism older and more rational than the substance of Debrett or Burke. He looked to the interest of the whole, and found that it lay in ever-wakeful conservative improvement.

When the war ended—at the summing-up of an epoch
of history—he asked his country to judge between the
Tories and the Opposition.

"On one side of the retrospect, to count nations
rescued and thrones re-established ; battles won with
matchless courage and triumphs unparalleled in their
splendour and consequences. They would see this little
island, after having saved the Continent, watch with a
steady guardian care over the tranquillity which it had
restored. They would have to enumerate, on the other
side of the account, a series of persevering objections to
every measure by which these glories and benefits have
been obtained ; a succession of theories refuted by facts
and of prophecies falsified by experience."

From experience, the last word, all his views seem
essentially to be derived ; experience, which the poet
drew as the arch bridging the generations. But Canning
never walked up the arch's outer side or spent all his
days gazing inward on the past : his eye was turned to
the outer gate, "wherethro' gleamed the untravelled
world" of a new society, to which Conservatism must
adjust itself or perish.

CROKER

CROKER

AMONG the bye-products of an ancient civilization science has found an interesting place for the "death-watch beetle." Ensconced in the oldest timbers of our finest buildings, sparing neither the inner shrines of religion nor the home of law, he presides over, if he does not directly assist in, the hidden decomposition of fabrics still seemingly unimpaired, and every year that he is left alone raises the bill for renovation. He asks one thing only as a condition of his well-being, an unventilated atmosphere ; admit a perpetual current of fresh air, and his powers are gone.

It must strike any student of long-lived institutions that this little animal has his human counterpart. When political or social fabrics fall into decay, a type of humanity will be found at their heart corresponding in all essentials to the beetle ; contributing, by their eleventh-hour agonies, to prolong the process of which they are symptoms ; blind, like animals long kept in darkness, when exposed to new light, and unable to understand the law of change. Sometimes clinging to lost ideals with the last Jacobites, sometimes sunk in the clay with Bubb Dodington, the harm they do is in strict proportion to their own virtue. Who can measure the damage inflicted on sane Conservatism by one reactionary of high character and personal charm ?

It is not with this branch of the species that we are concerned, in dealing with the wire-pullers of this life— the Henry Guys, the John Robinsons, and the Crokers. Their function is lower, but still fundamental. Through the long aphasia of the once eloquent Toryism of Pitt and Canning, Croker was high in the party's counsels. He was Peel's confidant for twenty years until, by betraying his party over Protection, Peel wantonly made the void which it took Disraeli another twenty years to fill. He often received or extracted confidences from Canning, Lyndhurst, and Wellington. He was the chief link between this Tory front bench and the Press. It was the day when the reviews governed political opinion, in a country (even after 1832) of a small electorate, classical education, and enviable leisure, and Croker was the *Quarterly's* sword-arm. He gave ninety-nine articles to its first hundred numbers, speedily replaced Southey as its offensive leader, and from 1811 till 1854 inspired its political direction. The leaders of the party approved, more often than not, his proof-sheets. His pages are the fruit of incessant hobnobbings, buttonholings, club dinners, country house gossip ; he has thoroughly stirred up the hive, he buzzes and stings like a king hornet of his class.

It is easy to exaggerate the real importance of politicians who keep diaries or write their memoirs, and it is particularly easy for themselves to do this. We know now that Bishop Burnet was not, as his History might suggest, indispensable to the military operations of William III ; just as Sir William Temple cannot be given, when his accounts are checked by others, the credit for making the

Triple Alliance. Those who have read the memoirs connected with the war of our own time will recall other instances of this tendency, which seems likely to be the last infirmity of western minds. But if for our knowledge of Croker we were reduced solely to the evidence of his enemies, there would still remain solid ground for saying that he must have a permanent place among the second-class makers of party.

His common reputation is low, for he was unlucky enough to quarrel with two uncommon men—with Macaulay and Disraeli, the greatest exponents of " in " and " out " fighting of the century. From these encounters this unhappy official emerged badly battered. Macaulay's essay on Croker's edition of Boswell, and the picture in " Coningsby " of the party hack Rigby, have the power of eating into our memories in youth, and refuse to be effaced, research we never so painfully. It proves impossible to forget that Rigby was " confided in by everybody, trusted by none," or that " to do the dirty work " was his " real business." Macaulay's letters teach us to hate Croker " like cold-boiled veal " ; that he was " a very bad man, a scandal to politics and letters." And though we learn that neither Macaulay's nor Disraeli's motives in these comments were wholly pure—though we find that their picture is a caricature, that Croker was a worthy family man, an eminent Secretary to the Admiralty, a friend to half the lame dogs of literature, and so respectable that he founded the Athenæum Club ; that his association with the " wicked " Lord Hertford, the original of Dizzy's " Monmouth " and Thackeray's Marquis of Steyne, had nothing dis-

E

creditable about it, all such certificates to character do not seem to dim the loud, clamorous colouring thrown on by the old masters. Indeed, even if (to borrow a word of Gibbon on Pope John XXIII) "the more scandalous charges were suppressed," Croker's character is not agreeable.

Some of his feats of literary pugilism form part of the history of that fancy. He was the *Quarterly's* instrument when it "killed John Keats"; he tried to divide Tennyson's skin when, as it turned out, the bear was very much alive. Lockhart, his last editor, with every opportunity for judgment and every party bias in his favour, has said harsh things of this tireless contributor; we could quote remarks more severe than "the bitterness of Gifford without his dignity, and the bigotry of Southey without his *bonne foi*." It is impossible to get away from the general spirit of distrust encircling him. We always return to Lytton Bulwer's impression, "the bald head and working mouth and dark, fine eyes, handsome enough in their way, but I would not trust them." With a score of kind actions and countless pieces of good advice to his credit, Croker never shook off the wire-puller's disease of considering persons, not humanity, and never escaped the wire-puller's doom of destroying the confidence which he so arduously sought.

His working creed can be gathered from his own lips. "Party is much the strongest passion of an Englishman's mind. Friendship, love, even avarice, give way before it." And party, which can rise to an embracing, generously-rooted confidence in men's deepest instincts, sinks in Croker to that congealed, time-restricted dogmatism characteristic of the Irish Protestantism whence he rose. He was one of those who ruin good causes by imputing bad motives, and hasten the swing of the pendulum by blackguarding the other side. His historical criticism was relevant enough when, as in Macaulay's case, it could fall upon a solid mass of one-sidedness, but it was monstrously incapable of separating finer issues or understanding a subtle and sensitive mind. His rough ostler's hand is seen at its worst in unloading his political prejudice upon a real historian like Mignet.

The adherents of this metallic, one-sided, "consistent" conversatism have one brass cymbal always tinkling in their mentality, and to its unvarying note they must prostrate themselves. On empirical grounds they may admit exception in detail, as Croker, who objurgated Parliamentary reform upon system, would allow it in proved scandals like Gatton or East Retford. But sound any new string—release any new breath of doctrine—and they hie back to the law and the prophets of their bosom, to individual property, or the Protestantism of the ever-consistent Reformers, or the invariable balancing of exports by imports. New aspects of truth are drowned in the clang of their venerable brass, the doors of their temples are banged and bolted. The booming gong in Croker's conventicle was the French Revolution. To that age, as born in 1780, he belonged. Its particular sequence of actions and reactions must, he argued, be true for all times and seasons. For the England of 1832, therefore, he prophesied revolution, followed by military dictatorship and "restoration"; in 1846, he could see no escape from the fall of all establishments, the repeal of the Union, and manhood suffrage. Frame a syllable of reasonable concession, and he retorts " the imbecile faction of the Gironde." Politics to his mind were a predestined diarchy between good and evil, Toryism and Reform, England and France.

To say that such predictions sometimes, or even often, have come true seems an irrelevancy. The worst of this semi-historical fatalism (for real history does not work in that way) is that it selects a panel of sequences ; those unfavourable to its case are rejected. Nor does *post hoc* become *propter hoc* simply because a few pessimists choose to say so. One is entitled to ask whether a corresponding amount of optimism might not have made all the difference, and to believe that a class which despairs of things does a good deal to bring things into a condition of despair.

Those frequenters of Canning clubs and Primrose League galas, who spend much time in denigrating symptoms of liberalism in their leaders, would do well to reflect that never were leaders so systematically undermined as Canning and Disraeli ; so far is it from being mathematically correct that the rank and file at a given moment is infallible. Croker, who for twenty years ignored Disraeli in public and maligned him in correspondence, did, it is true, ostensibly support Canning against Peel in the crisis of 1827 between Tories of the Right and Tory moderates. But he followed up his support with a homily to the effect that the *unum necessarium* was the aristocracy, and incited him, with lists of boroughmongers, to buy off the opposition of the Peers. He believed, in short, that the landed aristocracy then existent was the essence of the English State. As if, in the eye of English history, that aristocracy were not a parvenu ! As if English stability depended on accumulated rent-rolls ! This seemed to Croker the strongest point in his indictment of Peel's lapse over Protection : that it would extinguish the class who formed the core of the Constitution. He was wrong. If ever that great and proper cause of the landed interest should revive, its resurrection will not be in the eighteenth century dress, but in garments more integrally English, in character more original and popular, more deeply interfused with what another school of thought used to call " the good people of England."

A party is unhappy that takes its philosophy from the wisdom of the clubs, or from the aspiring climbers whom the Crokers typify. Walking the parks and St. James's, with jaunts to Brighton and the more comfortable homes of England, Croker merely megaphoned the post-prandial average opinion of men less intelligent than himself, and moulded the chance crumbs falling in off-moments from his leaders into a paste-like consistency, fit for general consumption. His supreme efforts were reserved for " keeping the party together," and by this he meant, as all his genus do, compromising the leaders' commitments and serving up a tasty dish, hot but non-committal, to the electors. If there is decent agreement on the bridge (so they argue) and a jazz band in the saloon, the ship is well found, though the look-out man may be asleep and a compartment flooded in the hold.

He extended this programme of irascible stationariness to the philosophy of Toryism, which he found to consist

in "stability," and in the majestic wronged name of
Burke he recognized its prophet. It is almost impossible
to over-paint the devastating legacy left to nineteenth-
century Conservatism by this use of the Burke formula.
The passive obedience given by their great-grandfathers
to Church and King was now transferred to this Irish
reformer ; the verbal inspiration, which their grandsons
have found to survive in the Protestant Bible, they conceded to the anti-Jacobin.   It was in the name of Burke
that modern Conservatives refused to amend an unwork-
able Constitution ; in Burke's name they denied the full
measure of religious toleration, and covered with his
mantle the sins of the worst property owners.   But even
omitting the vast difference between the early and the
aged Burke, and the unveracious selection of a part only
of a great man's works, one must urge that these arbitrary
disciples have missed his most essential teaching—that
circumstances are the heart of every political problem.   A
leader who never ceased to upbraid naked, abstract, un-
clothed dogmatisms, is invoked to justify a static theory
and the glory of things as they are, and his case against a
particular revolution is twisted into attack on any movement at all.

If it cannot be gleaned from Burke, though we think
it can, it is yet legitimate to believe that not " stability "
but the proved interest of the whole is the core of Toryism
—a faith (so far as it is consciously held) based not on
present prejudices so much as on the entire history of the
realm.   For the worst of " things as they are " is that it
means in practice " things as they were yesterday " ; the
official vision of the conventional retrospects no farther.

A calamity ; for though it is morally certain that we are wiser than our fathers, it is doubtful whether we are more profound than all the ages. So it is that there lies more hope for present-day England in the practice of the Elizabethans than in the Cobden Club publications or the literature of the Primrose League. Croker, we may add, adjured Peel in 1834 to give youth a chance, but when it came to facts he had uncommonly little use for " Young England."

On a special and immediate issue the views of the Crokers may, of course, prove their worth ; they shine in narrow streets. On the whole, the most pathetic incident in this unpathetic life was his breach with Peel, whom he loved only less than the Corn Laws, and we can hardly read their letters without disliking the leader who so sharply dropped his twenty years' " Ever yours affectionately " for " Sir, I have the honour." In 1841, Croker had, under Peel's inspiration, stated the Conservative case for moderate reform of the tariff, based upon protection for agriculture ; it was Peel who in 1846 expected him, and the whole party, to eat his words. In the *Quarterly* article that underlined this betrayal, Croker's ability to state a brief was well seen. The fallacy of the ground taken, that a famine in Irish potatoes made it imperative to open England to foreign corn, and that a temporary emergency must be met with a permanent surrender ; the iniquitous preparation and concealment of the change ; the retaking of office, ostensibly to keep out the Radicals and Cobden, whom three months later he was to smother with eulogy—on all this the indictment is massive, comparatively reasonable, and unanswerable. The protectionist party was, as he feared, gone—lapsing for a season, as it is apt to, down to sterilities of capitalism and No Popery.

But it is not in home truths on isolated questions that the vital spirit of a party consists—more especially if such truths are complicated with the interests of one class. " Damn him," said Melbourne of one who began canvassing for Pitt's vacant seat before Pitt was buried, " can nothing but party enter that cold heart ? " Some at least of those who have led the Tories to great enduring success have spoken of a " national party," and commended their party to the nation by putting the nation first. The Crokers of Conservatism do their best to impede this fusion ; embedded in their hard-bitten righteousness, they think to resist by negation the evil they have failed to conciliate. Croker, from his youth up, believed in the justice of Catholic emancipation, but when in 1829 the matter came up for decision, then he refused to concede to " intimidation " what he had granted on the merits. We know too well this phenomenon. Grievances are admitted and allowed to accumulate till they explode ; and then those who have sat on the safety valve ask us all to sit on bayonets. The mess which Conservatives have refused to handle thus becomes a matter of " prestige," of " loyalty," and all the other gags of Stupidity-street ; the facts you refused to face, but which taken earlier would have been malleable and curable by lenitives, rise up now as a brick wall, as " intimidation " and dishonour ; against which, last stage of all, these narrow foreheads dash themselves, till it falls in rubble and destruction—for them, for theirs, and for many

better than they. Croker, let it be conceded despite
Macaulay, was an honourable man : did he not get the
Elgin marbles for the nation, nearly get Cleopatra's
Needle, and quite found the Athenæum ? So are they all,
all honourable men. But the finest subaltern material in
the world can lead armies to destruction, and it takes
more than respectable men to control national destinies.
It has been seen before now what one great mind can do
to galvanize a whole party, as it has been proved super-
abundantly that the rank and file cannot command.
Conceive the state of England if the mass of the House of
Commons had really ruled in 1660, in 1715, or later dates
one could mention—the mass who refused Parliamentary
reform to Pitt and threw out the income-tax in 1815.
Have we not suffered enough from the excellent men who
quote Burke against the supertax, whose minds turn
fondly to halcyon days when British soldiers danced
round the Taj—whose philosophy is the thin end of
wedges, and their religion the arid, parade-ground
Protestantism of the public school ?

If Conservatism is a matter of adjusting leaders and
planks, by all means let us nail Croker to us ; he is
tough wood and has no blurred edges. If it can be
comprised in a frenzy, we can soak ourselves in the
" Regicide Peace " ; if in the toasts of Ulster, we can
explore with Froude the integrity of Anne Boleyn and the
undying creed of racial superiority. But if, like other
party faiths, it is a means to an end—if it is a way of
looking at life that is only justified if it makes life better—
then we shall cease to harp upon a single string, to entrust
ourselves to a single name, or listen with Croker to the

echoes of a single class sounding the galleries of Mayfair and the shires. We are obliged, doubtless, to take our political faith upon a balance of advantages, and to follow the leaders who best preserve that balance as a whole. But it is not the leaders of Conservatism who have often brought it to ruin.

If it were possible to enlarge our phylacteries a little less and our historic consciousness a little more, we should think that Liberalism is Conservatism in the making, and that Toryism is the Liberalism of the past ; we should become less certain that we, standing at one notch of eddying time, hold in its purity the entire faith given to the Churches. We can be more confident of finding a philosophy in the past—rooted in the soil, in the facts of a growing national society, not sectional, but in tune with the common aspirations which our history shows Englishmen have cherished. This history may remind us that our Church and Constitution have flourished just in proportion as they have been broad and elastic, and that those who have tried to narrow them have failed.

A long farewell, then, to this earthy narrowing Croker, type and exemplar of so many honourable men. He tried to stabilize, to cabin and confine us ; we have burst out of these cere-clothes, and still Toryism survives. We have done with the Regent, with the Grenvilles, the gold plate, and the incredible game laws ; our belief is no more meted out to us by the *Quarterly*, or regulated in the ambit of St. James's. The " ins " and the " outs " of the forties, heated with port and class-consciousness, encumber us no longer. Even in their day a way of escape was opening, a hope of something broad, cool, and unanathematizing—a way sounded from distant places, whence the Lake poets and the school of Newman were recalling England to a more universal conservatism and a catholic heritage. Which still may be ours.

SOUTHEY AND WORDSWORTH

SOUTHEY AND WORDSWORTH

WHEN George the Magnificent was Regent and King, Southey as Poet Laureate was official head of English letters, and in common, even in uncommon opinion, best represented the Lake school. To the Disraeli of 1833 he seemed "the greatest man of the age," to Byron or Hazlitt he was the archapostate; high and dry Anglicanism reckoned him as chief pillar of the Church. Except for a few duty Odes, produced not without assistance from doses of magnesia, he had abandoned poetry, but his achievement in prose was ceaseless, omniscient, and formally almost perfect. It would be hard to find purer models of narrative than his lives of Nelson (for which he received thanks in person from the *ingénue* Princess Victoria), of Cowper and of Wesley—than the *Colloquies*, or *The Book of the Church*, while his *Quarterly* essays, broad in sweep, dogmatic and pointed, justly appealed for twenty-five years to the gentlemen of England. A pension, remuneration of £100 an article, the offers of a baronetcy and of the editorial chair of *The Times*, measure his political services to the Tories.

A quarter of a century had gone by since young Southey, already a Stoic and a republican, had been ejected from Westminster, rejected at Christ Church and received at Balliol ; since he and Coleridge (gently

71

removed from the 15th Light Dragoons) had planned to transport themselves and the two Misses Fricker to the Susquehanna, there to energise an agricultural colony on principles of fraternity ; since the young Wordsworth had been dogged by Pittite spies and had found love in Girondin France.   By the 'thirties these fiery furnaces were out.   Southey at Keswick was annotating from 14,000 volumes the inevitable doom of revolution ; the owner of Rydal had become successively a militiaman, a revenue official, and a justice of the peace ; from the cloud-encompassed hill of Highgate, Coleridge was conversing upon the timeless conservatism of the Deity. Yet it would be fallacious to ascribe their disillusionment wholly to senility, love of place, or power of common opinion, and far more so to ignore its political instruction. For the Lake poets, unlike Burke, learned their revolution by experience ; they had ascended into its high places, and seen the kingdoms of the world fouled by anarchs. If conservatism survived to keep democracy partially safe for the next century, all three " Lakers " share in the achievement.

Southey, the one ordinary mortal of this extraordinary band, can be dissected in bald prose.   One of those thin, energetic, noisy men who love cats, puns, and controversial writings, there is something parched and unkind about his virtue.   The quiet conviction of immortal fame, which Dante or Milton could wear as a toga, sits rather absurdly on him, and we are naturally unimpressed by the boasted blows he promises to deal the Satanic Byron.   His exhausting cheerfulness in early life, like his later gloom, seems to expose a purely physical basis of vitality, which expired after years of mechanical literary toil, leaving a dim light in the socket. Few who have held so high a place have had so little intrinsic wisdom. No one who has reached middle age will upbraid a public man for the mere changing his mind, but Southey passed violently from one pole or extremity to the other, never relating his revisions to the facts as a whole. His prejudices, once acquired, became physical obsessions ; from some particular evil he must always generalize to universal calamity ; he is a master of the *post hoc propter hoc* method, that worst vice of argumentation. On major issues he was ever in the wrong ; he was an anti-bullionist, an anti-Catholic, an anti-Reformer ; he wished the repeal of Fox's Libel Act, and he thought in 1814 that France should lose more territory. He was one of those unhappy publicists who can find no public man to their liking, save one who is irretrievably dead. Pouring scorn on the administration and the memory of Pitt, he was dissatisfied with Fox and disappointed in Canning ; only the admirable but assassinated Percival reached his standard. There are too many femininities of epithet about his political criticism—" the Futilitarians," " the Noddles," and the like, and too many surpassing perversities, as that only the missionaries would save India for Britain. The dedication of his collected essays to Sir Robert Inglis (the chosen representative of Protestant Oxford to replace the renegade Robert Peel) shows with what difficulty the pious recluse can escape becoming a pious prig ; " we who know in Whom we believe "—such effusions are akin to his view, which was almost a hope, of a cholera epidemic about to smite an apostate nation. In sum,

F

Southey lived for forty years in a wilderness with an adoring community of cats and mortals, a library, and commonplace books ; his rare visits to London or the Continent, and his prolific correspondence with friends and relations (from which filial piety has selected for us ten volumes) were no substitute for the full tide of human existence.

But enough of detraction. A patient reading must always end in affection for this man of real virtue, while the very average vicissitudes of his character make him in some ways a figure of more political significance than the two men of genius whose glory surrounds him. That regular pen brought bread not to his own children only, but to those of Coleridge ; his hand was ever open to help men of letters who needed it ; he can be acquitted, in an age of literary savagery, of private rancour or seeking strife. He was by temperament the only man of action of his school ; his love of country bore the wear of daily life better than Wordsworth's—the historian of Nelson and the Peninsular War felt with what majesty the men in the ranks could fight. A photographic power of mind marked from his first days the actual woes of society, and while Coleridge was distilling ecstasy or abasement from opium, Southey was trying to heal poverty in correspondence with Owen and Sadler.

Given a compound of Southey's intense purity, sensitiveness, and mercurial conviction, some sharp reaction from the Revolution was certain. Bonaparte, not Burke, turned the Lake poets into conservatives. France had played traitor to liberty, and nowhere more so than in the lands Southey of all Englishmen knew best—Spain and Portugal. On this matter above all, he fell foul of the Whigs ; " when Bonaparte would persuade the French that the conquest of Spain and Portugal is easy, and the ruin of England certain, his surest policy is to fill the *Moniteur* with the speeches of a party leader, the cowardly sophistry of a party critic, and the fallacies and falsehoods of an Opposition paper."

He derived two further conclusions from the revolutionary era. Two years of travel in Portugal and ten years of the Irish question embued him with a hatred of the Papacy. If he had been born a century earlier or later, he must surely have become an Anglican prelate. As it was, a child of the late eighteenth century, he had refused to take orders and passed through pantheism to a sort of Christian quietude ; if Rome offended his reason and the Revolution his heart, what form of institutionalism was elastic enough to include this exacting idealistic patriot ? Stamped still deeper into his consciousness was the association of cruelty and violence with " the mob," and he believed now that sheer anarchy must follow any public recognition of the rights of man. The real Terror at Paris had obliterated his hopes of France ; a pinchbeck Pittite terror at home had maimed his ideals for England. " Whether the fiend," he wrote later, " who bestrides it and spurs it on, have Jacobin or Anti-Jacobin written in his forehead, the many-headed beast is the same." By a more prosaic route than his friends, Southey at this stage had come to the same conclusion, that the statesman must substitute morals for rights, obedience for will, and character for expediency.

Till 1811, and at heart perhaps even beyond that date, he clung to many reforming views. " The political system of Christianity," which he had meant to realize in America, he still hoped to find, though on a changed plan. In 1808, he declares himself to be of " the school of Sydney, and Hutchinson, and Milton " ; in 1814, he hoped against the Bourbons' restoration, and would be a republican, were England fit for such liberty. He had spoken of " the ineffaceable infamy of bombarding Copenhagen," and called for the liberalizing of South America. He saw no alternatives for England, but ruin or constitutional reform.

But by 1812 the combination of menace from foreign enemies and from the English Radical Left had worked its usual havoc in consolidating the English Right ; Cobbett, Burdett, and Orator Hunt had completed the work of Bonaparte. Southey was convinced that Press licence would make possible the revolution which the democrats desired, and that drastic reform of the franchise would mean a Convention. Up to 1816 at least he was ready to grant some concession to freeholders and copyholders, and some representation to the great towns, but he began to argue that such legislation, even if innocuous, was of very secondary importance to moral and administrative energy. With advancing age and mental inbreeding, a half-light of pessimism darkened his eyes, that once had seen man and his future in such sanguine colours. He demanded more repression and transportation, discovered in Anglicanism the only city of refuge, and sank at last into something indistinguishable from timorous other-worldliness.

If pre-Reform England had listened to all that Southey wrote, and not only to the meaner part of it, enormous evil would have been spared to their own age and to ours. For though those who see politics, not through reason but the heart, may end in apparent reaction as a means to save what they love, anything they do see is real and poignant. It was Southey's achievement to perceive that nothing could perpetuate England as she stood between 1815 and 1830, and that nothing ought to. He saw that the condition of the people cried to heaven ; that " there can be no safety with a population half Luddite, half Lazzaroni." In an image of frightful truth he compared the submerged classes of the new industrialism to the dogs of Constantinople, " a nuisance to the community while they live, and dying miserably at last." With the teachers of his youth, he thought that man was by nature virtuous, and good principle native within us, and therefore attributed responsibility for revolutions to bad government. Refusing to swallow the iron draughts of Malthus, he found the root of the trouble in the quack remedies, the accumulated sins and omissions, of the ruling class.

The " morbid change " in England was immediately due, in his opinion, to industrialism ; to Adam Smith, and his " tedious and hard-hearted book "—to that negation of government which had deprived the poor of their hope, the essential salt of a commonwealth. From the moment of the peace in 1815, he implored the legislators not to be drowned under the false cry of retrenchment, but to discharge their debt to those who had fought by giving them work. The State should assist emigration, colonize the empty spaces of England, check enclosure, and set up Savings banks. He hoped, vainly as it happened, that Canning would rouse himself to remodel the Poor-law, and pleaded for public work as against doles. He examined with candour and sympathy the activities of Spence, the land nationalizer, and of Robert Owen, and approved the first rudiments of the co-operative movement. No man better illustrates the reality of that never-yet wholly severed link between one sort of Tory and one sort of Socialist. Prison reform, law reform, licensing, the game-laws, adulteration, limitation of entail, heavier income-tax, restoration of parish government, a federal Empire—for twenty years Southey preached these things, in and out of season, to a generation of Tories worn by war and hag-ridden by economics. But it is not unusual for that party to stop their ears against their prophets.

Laissez-faire was to him principally the sin against society, and he was not prepared to compromise, like Peel or Russell, with " the cool calculating inhumanity " of the cotton kings. As he saw it, both cause and remedy lay far deeper than economics. If the cause of pauperism were " misfortune in one instance, misconduct in fifty," a true government (not one of " Noddles " like Liverpool's, which he thought " deficient in everything except good intentions ") would bulwark by reform the native goodness of the English people. They would even go beyond the practical remedies Southey had urged, and recognise by their action that virtue and happiness are the ingredients of States. It is immaterial, for us at least, that Southey was speaking rather as an Anglican than a sociologist. It is enough that he saw that gain, "the principle of our social system," was "awfully opposed to the spirit of Christianity." Only by education, and that on Christian principle, could he see a chance of reconciling the two things which he desired to unite, "Conservation and Improvement."

Macaulay, the young master of false antithesis and contemporary optimism, pounced upon Southey's *Colloquies*, and scarified his supposed ideal of an "omniscient and omnipotent State"; those who reflect upon our social history during the next century may judge between them.

> "All that the world's coarse thumb
> And finger failed to plumb "

in the heyday of Macaulay and Bright, all this may rise up and call Southey blessed. Embedded in tracts of aridity or gloom, the oases stand out in the huge area of his writing—not all mirage, but with here and there a tree for healing, here and there water at which posterity may quench its thirst.

"I have no respect whatever for Whigs," said Wordsworth in old age, "but I have a great deal of the Chartist in me." Making the due allowances, the greater man did pass through much the same political cycle as Southey, and though the Chartist element needs research to find it, something of the sort is there. At least it is permissible to question the worth of some modern criticism, which bifurcates the poet's life and ascribes some poetic decline of later years to a loss of ideal, proved by acceptance of government pay or the patronage of Lord Lonsdale. Actually, the " beastly and pitiful wretch" pilloried by Shelley never, I think, turned apostate to his vow of 1811 :

> " That an accursed thing it is to gaze
> On prosperous tyrants with a dazzled eye."

But whatever the consistency of the teaching, it was always of higher calibre and more resonant depth than that we have gathered from Southey.

Far more than any of his friends, Wordsworth had staked his soul on the truth of the Revolution, and the nemesis of his faith was a process infinitely more torturing and intolerable. He had traversed France in the first flush of fraternity ; he had thought of dedicating his life to that cause ; his first earthly child, his first spiritual visions, were born in France. The decline of France into butchery and imperialism broke for ten years the thread of his life ; between that, and what he viewed as Pitt's despotism, he wandered like an outcast, finding nothing on earth except " the noble living and the noble dead." Even *The Prelude*, written between 1799 and 1805, shows that his reaction owed nothing substantial to events after Waterloo ; compressed and agonizing, it was also complete. He had been too early a child of Nature to endure a gross loss of identity between Nature and plain morals, or the dominion of men who claimed by bare reason to verify Nature's rights. An unspanned gulf lay between the executioners on the Seine or the Loire, and his Cumberland " statesmen," armed in their primitive excellence and " pure religion breathing household laws." France had cast herself down the steep places with many swine.

" The life in the soul," as the memorable Cintra essay puts it, " has been directly and mortally warred against " ; reason " had abominations to endure in her inmost sanctuary."

The poet, crowning himself like Dante, had early attained conviction of his high calling. No " unreasoning herd " could lay laws upon him, for " the poet binds together by passion and knowledge the vast empire of human society." All the deeper fundamentals of his teaching, all the germs of *Prelude* and *Excursion*, are in the preface of 1800 to *Lyrical Ballads*. He desired to record " the primary laws of our nature," " the great and simple affections of our nature," and to do this with permanence of speech which was impossible in the artificiality of great cities. Amid all contradictions of reason and fluctuating opinion, he was seeking the permanent—" the central peace subsisting at the heart of endless agitation."

Formerly, in France, he had followed nature unreflectingly, and filled his eyes with genial pleasure, " as if life's business were a summer mood." Tragedy and suffering had taught him that human reason, if abstracted from love, duty, and circumstance, determined no right and provided no happiness. The riddle of the universe was not to be read by a faculty dealing in " minute and speculative pains " ; the constancy of the imaginative will alone could bear with, and master, the facts of life. A philosophy of sensual experience,

> " One that would peep and botanize
> Upon his mother's grave " ;

the rationalist—

> " One to whose smooth-rubbed soul can cling
> Nor form, nor feeling, great nor small ;
> A reasoning self-sufficient thing,
> An intellectual all in all " ;

neither of these could make harmony of " the still sad music of humanity." God had never abandoned man " to feel the weight of his own reason " ; " nature's gradual processes " were not caught in a sudden glory by one short generation ; yet it was impossible, on the other hand, that truth and virtue had been made

> " Hard to be won, and only by a few,"

and denied for ever to the lowly, the oppressed, the inexorably deprived.

Not so—and here Wordsworth re-echoes a vital doctrine of the greatest mystic conservative of the seventeenth century, Henry Vaughan—

> " The primal duties shine aloft, like stars ;
> The charities that soothe, and heal, and bless,
> Are scattered at the feet of man, like flowers."

Duty for men, children of God, will be found in the common road ; duties and rights must be fixed in the lasting scheme of things, open to the humble, but concealed from the arrogance of reason. The poet thus approaches the conclusion of Oliver Cromwell, the Calvinist ; " we have found the cause of God by the works of God, which are the testimony of God."

Live then, he says, according to nature, but nature as read in her lasting works. Go close to her, in places where she is easily to be found ; you will find the child is father to the man, and all generations bound close by natural piety. Men may pass, but

> " The form remains, the function never dies."

Nature " matures her processes by steadfast laws," and the mass of creation springs in articulated progress from creeping things up to the moralized man. Variety and degree are of her ordaining ; as " similitude in dissimilitude " is the test of moral æsthetic, so

> " The shifting aims,
> The moral interests, the creative might,
> The varied functions and high attributes
> Of civil action "

cannot be smothered, or down-levelled, by tyranny and mobs. The poet shares, then, in that anti-intellectuality, that scepticism as to the merit of unaided mind, which is found in all transcended conservatives, in Vaughan, in Newman, or in Burke. He found in reason too much " power and energy detached from moral purpose " ; book knowledge would always " neglect the universal heart "—it must be brought to its proper and final test,

> " Life, human life, with all its sacred claims
> Of sex and age, and heaven-descended rights."

Nature, so passive, so majestical, is falsified, he tells us, and her code distorted by the critical intellect. Moral judgment, and " this alone is genuine liberty," has something of resignation in it. Those who have attained it accept their place in a great scheme ;

> " Willing to work and to be wrought upon,"

they maintain in themselves the law of existence, and poise the balance " of action from without and from within." But the teaching of this pure transcendentalist can never finally lead to passive obedience. His very revolt, alike from eighteenth-century convention and revolutionary abstraction, sprang from their suppression of individual worth ; human personality is the base to his philosophy of right, which rests on a God-given equality of soul and a moral liberty to which all may ascend. His virtue is an active principle ; you must give something to Nature, or you can never receive; the Happy Warrior and the old Leech-gatherer go hard to their work. Logically, Wordsworth could, therefore, denounce the new manufacturing system, which deprived the poor of self-subsistence and the joy of mutual help. Man was not born to be " a tool or implement " ; any " discipline of virtue " made it incumbent on the State to educate all her members.

It is easy enough to frame an indictment against the Lake poets' politics—to depict this mystic in old age manufacturing freeholders for the Lonsdales, evolving his *Ecclesiastical Sonnets*, and sharing at large in the shovel-hatted politics of Southey. But compare their teaching, in hope for the future, with the Conservatism of Eldon, of Scott, even of Canning, or even of Burke, and the superiority of their basis, in the scale of enduringness, is surely manifest. The lawyer may become sterile, the historian static, even the empirical genius mistake prejudice for principle, but those who, with all mistakes, stand on the moral law are never far removed from the principle of growth. Their fire is never extinct, a strong wind may set the embers glowing.

COLERIDGE

COLERIDGE

CANNING, said the subject of this essay, "flashed such a light around the constitution, that it was difficult to see the ruins of the fabric through it." On this unreformed England, the full limits of whose beneficent powers Canning had exhausted, Coleridge turned for thirty years the intermittent blaze of his vast, trained, betrayed, intelligence. The results for English Conservative thought have not always been adequately recognized. Hazlitt said truly that he had a tangential mind, and the drip, drip, of his oracles, spray flying in all directions, wears away the most rock-like patience. And much of his clearest thought—if one can ever mention clearness of Coleridge—lies embedded in the *Friend*, the odd periodical issued from Keswick in 1809-10 which, overlaid by masses of dubious metaphysic and tiresome anecdote, wore out the subscribers within eight months.

But the spiritual directors of Victorian England all acknowledge his influence. The debt of Wordsworth goes without saying. Carlyle, who disliked his theology and resented sitting as "a passive bucket" to another seer's deliverance, yet did justice to "this memorable man," to "the piercing radiances," the "glorious islets," which rose at rare intervals out of the general haze. Newman confessed that this peculiar apostle laid "a

philosophical basis " for the Oxford movement, for he
" made trial of his age, and succeeded in interesting its
genius in the cause of Catholic truth." Maurice and the
Christian Socialists took half of his ideas, Maine and the
historical school adopted the doctrine of development
which he was first to import from Germany. The most
judicial thinker of the century, John Mill, joins him with
Bentham as " the two great seminal minds of England
in their age," and terms him the first real philosopher of
conservatism. The more closely the lasting values of
Conservatism are studied, or the further men depart from
the traditional sectarianism of Conservative formulas, so
much the deeper will become the influence of Coleridge.
To welcome and absorb that teaching, one type of conservative mind will never be unready. For on a broad view
of the whole historic body of Conservative politics in this
country, it would appear that now and at all times it has
comprised two main sub-divisions, as distinct as bodies
can be which are composed of elements, in themselves,
complex and indivisible ; if we call the one Conservative
and the other Tory, the definition, though open to doubt,
will convey the distinction. The first, at any rate, has
borne on its nominal roll names like Clarendon, Blackstone, Eldon, or Peel, and its function has been to defend
the existing order. Sometimes it has claimed that this
order was divinely begotten, at others it has anchored the
cause to some specific group of human ordinances like
the Revolution of 1688, at a later date has found in some
one principle, such as the sanctity of property, the
shibboleth which tells false men from true. Its adherents
have drawn upon religion, law, history, and science, to

vindicate things established, and found in Burke their new Messiah.

The second school are those who have performed the pioneer task of bridging the party over the intellectual and political revolutions of the last two hundred years. Harley and Bolingbroke, Pitt and Canning, Young England and Disraeli ; such is the type in outward affairs. Their leaders have often done radical things from inside the conservative frame, and were ceaselessly attacked by their followers as a consequence. They seem to have thought less of the present than of the future. They viewed their party less as representing the dominant classes of the present than as standing for the most per-manent, and hence the most vital and entirely natural, interests of the people as a whole. They recognised, it would seem, that this national heritage must necessarily find very differing interpretation in different ages, and therefore that conservatism consisted less in maintaining fixed institutions than in acting in tune with the conserva-tive spirit. When, accordingly, they pruned the abuses of one age with unsparing hand, they reverted to the first and permanent principles of conservatism, and looked behind the institutions of their own generation for the spirit of the nation which gave them life.

It was to this latter sort of Conservative doctrine that Coleridge made his own profound and subtle contribu-tion. Like Burke, the great man of the other school, he did his work under the shadow of the French Revolution, but unlike Burke he had the fate or the felicity to outlive it. If the contrast is to be justly drawn one must remem-ber that in 1789 Burke was a worn man of sixty, Coleridge a boy of seventeen, "when to be young was very heaven." With Southey and Wordsworth, he was seized by the promised reign of natural virtue, and planned to escape from selfish individualist civilisation to communist perfection by the Susquehanna. Like them he pronounced the first war against France to be iniquitous, and prolonged his criticism of Pitt beyond the grave. Yet from 1794 onwards he was denouncing the Jacobins, and for the enlightened, sobered, wisdom of Conservatism upon the subject of the Revolution, men will turn from the heated hysterical pages of Burke's *Reflections* to the voice from the Lakes. One of Coleridge's firmest convictions, partly derived perhaps from his intimacy with Milton and the Commonwealth men (whom he called " the stars of that narrow interspace of blue sky between the black clouds of the first and second Charles' reigns ") was that truth is found out by conflict—that every speculative error, if strongly held by good men, must have its golden side. No one has shown more strongly the boomerang danger that comes of using any stick to belabour one's opponents, and he has a searching criticism of Burke's versatility of principle. " If his opponents are theorists, then everything is to be founded on prudence, on mere calculations of expediency ; and every man is represented as acting according to the state of his own immediate self-interest. Are his opponents calculators ? Then calculation itself is represented as a sort of crime. God has given us feelings, and we are to obey them, and the most absurd prejudices become venerable, to which these feelings have given consecration."

As for the Revolution, " to hope too boldly of human

nature "—the fault of the youthful revolutionary—" is a
fault which all good men have an interest in forgiving."
" Angry misrepresentations," " to represent a political
system as having no charm but for robbers and assassins "
—all this, he urged, merely drove into the enemy's camp
those idealists who might be won for the Conservative
garrison.

The Pitt system, on which Cobbett used so freely his
undiscriminating bludgeon, is still in a real sense too
near to us for an agreed appraisement ; it touches on too
many social nerves that are still tender, it brings into dis-
pute the very end of society.   Conservatives who cannot
accept the facile view of a " fiendish," or stony-hearted,
minister will, however, at this time of day be disposed to
admit that the panic, and the ensuing repressive legislation, of 1794-99 were both carried much too far.   If so,
they will appreciate the amount of stern home truth in
Coleridge's criticism of the ruling class.   " Instead of
contenting themselves with opposing the real blessings of
English law to the splendid promises of untried theory, too
large a part of those, who called themselves Anti-Jacobins,
did all in their power to suspend those blessings, and thus
furnished new arguments to the advocates of innovation,
when they should have been answering the old ones."
By defending " the most disgusting forms of despotism "
in Europe, they endangered the monarchy at home.
Worse still, " they justified the corruptions of the State
by the same vague arguments of general reason, with
which the State itself had been attacked by the Jacobins ";
" to withstand the arguments of the lawless, they ob-
scured the general light of the law, that spies and infor-

mers might tyrannise and escape in the ominous darkness." In the teeth of facts, they roused the hue and
cry of " property," and at last " ended in believing their
own lie, even as our bulls in Borrowdale sometimes run
mad with the echo of their own bellowing."

On the social policy, or lack of it, during the last
phase of the war and the middle stage of the Industrial
revolution, there is, unluckily, less ground for difference
of opinion. But here Coleridge spoke, as few on his side
of politics were to speak till Shaftesbury and Disraeli.
Radicalism, he pointed out, represented the inevitable
revenge of the neglected poor. " When the government
and the aristocracy of this country had subordinated
persons to things, and treated the one like the other—the
poor, with some reason, and almost in self-defence,
learned to set up rights above duties." He was unable to
exhibit the other-worldliness of the Wilberforce school, in
face of this morass of social misery : " can we wonder
that men should want humanity, who want all the circumstances of life that humanize ? " Nor could he find
conviction, like most of Liverpool's cabinet, in the
maxims of *laisser-faire*. He was told that " all things
find their level." " But persons," he repeats, " are not
things ; but man does not find his level." After a
spell of long semi-starvation, or of unemployment, all
things are not as they were before ; " neither in body nor
in soul does the man find his level." The English
enclosures, or the Highland evictions, may each, on a
balance sheet, have added to the sum of national wealth,
but not intrinsically, for men " ought to be weighed, not
counted." He disputed the very first elements of cheap-

ness as policy. " You talk about making this article
cheaper by reducing its price in the market from 8d. to
6d. But suppose, in so doing, you have rendered your
country weaker against a foreign foe ; suppose you have
demoralized thousands of your fellow-countrymen, and
have sown discontent between one class of society and
another, your article is tolerably dear, I take it, after all."
The sum of English riches was nothing apart from its
distribution.   " We have game laws, corn laws, cotton
factories, Spitalfields, the tillers of the land paid by poor
rates, and the remainder of the population mechanized
into engines for the manufactory of new rich men ; yea,
the machinery of the wealth of the nation made up of the
wretchedness, disease, and depravity of those who should
constitute the strength of the nation."   What healing
could the Whig remedy of franchise reform, what did
the rule of law, bring for this growing fissure of rich
and poor into two nations ? " It is a mockery of our
fellow creatures' wrongs to call them equal in rights,
when by the bitter compulsion of their wants we make
them inferior to us in all that can soften the heart, or
dignify the understanding."

Such extreme sensitiveness to the claims of humanity
gives all the greater force to his wholesale repudiation of
Jacobinism. He found the roots of this evil system in the
deduction of all men's social rights from Reason, in
respect of which all men are equal. There is, he admits,
" a potential divinity in every man," and freedom of the
will is the essence of morality. But Rousseau's followers
transferred this internal moral rule, which binds the
conscience, to regulate the everyday life of man who is

" something besides reason." The purity of the " general will " can be only a matter of probability, and the theory is the confusion of moral, or religious, with political claims. It " confounds the sufficiency of the conscience to make every person a moral and amenable being, with the sufficiency of judgment and experience requisite to the exercise of political right." Its logical consequences heightened its absurdity. For this identity of reason would validate only one form of constitution, but " a constitution equally suited to China and America, or to Russia and Great Britain must, surely, be equally unfit for both." In a word, " by this system the observation of times, places, relative bearings, national customs and character, is rendered superfluous " ; and " by the magic oracles of certain axioms and definitions it is revealed how the world with all its concerns should be mechanized, and then let go on of itself."

One portion of this criticism springs direct from a disputable point in Coleridge's philosophy—the distinction between the reason and the understanding. But his religion accounts for more. Bare reason was, in his eyes, the fatal fruit by which our first father fell, or the harlot goddess who prostituted the Revolution. " It is the science of cosmopolitism without country, of philanthropy without neighbourliness or consanguinity, in short, of all the impostures of that philosophy of the French Revolution, which would sacrifice each to the shadowy idol of all." He shared, also, Canning's horror of efforts to embody abstractions. The economists, he declared, did sacrifice to a juggernaut State : " what is this Society, this Whole, this State ? Is it anything else but a

word of convenience, to express at once the aggregate
of confederated individuals living in a certain
district ? "

All this sort of reasoning, much of which he held in
common with Burke, he pushed much further, till he is
found at length to be attacking all that Burke had lived
by. Over and over again he makes the point, that a
scheme of thought, in politics or elsewhere, must be
taken as a whole. " I have no objection," he told his
Highgate audience in the last year of his life, " to your
aspiring to the political principles of our old Cavaliers ;
but embrace them all fully, and not merely this and that
feeling, whilst in other points you speak the canting
foppery of the Benthamite or Malthusian schools."
Disregarding the epithets, there is, surely, a deep political
truth here. One tree will not yield both figs and thistles,
and one social system cannot, for example, protect pro-
duction but abandon exchange to non-interference ;
that is, not indefinitely. Coleridge was not content,
therefore, to attack the superficial fortifications of the
Revolution, but concentrated his energy against the
mighty foundations deep below the soil. He held that
a people cannot think radically and yet retain conservative institutions : it would be seen, " whether a fancied
superiority to their ancestors' intellects must not speedily
be followed, in the popular mind, by disrespect for their
ancestors' institutions."

The cause of authority could not be long defended on
the philosophy of Locke ; it offered, he thought, no
strong buckler against " the prurient, bustling, and
revolutionary " French teaching. The aged parent was

unable to resist the onslaught of her lineal heir. To this mechanical philosophy and its material twin, the Revolution of 1688, he devoted a gloomy page of summary in the *Friend*—elaborated in weaker form in *Church and State*. " A system of natural rights instead of social and hereditary privileges ; the feeling of being an historical people, generation linked to generation by ancestral reputation, by tradition, by heraldry—this noble feeling, I say, openly stormed or perilously undermined " ; " an Ouran Outang theology " ; " our state policy a Cyclops with one eye, and that in the back of the head ; our measures become either a series of anachronisms, or a truckling to events." So much for negative criticism ; and we must come to those " spectral Puseyisms, monstrous illusory Hybrids, and ecclesiastical Chimæras " of his which, moans Carlyle, " now roam the earth in a very lamentable manner " ; that is, to whatever survives in Coleridge, or may be found in any poet, of positive political idea.

One remark alone shows that he has left the eighteenth century behind him : it is that " nothing great was ever achieved without enthusiasm." The particular application was to point a contrast between Peel, " who is rather remarkable for groundless and unlucky concessions," and the democratic leaders of that age. The first always addressed himself to special interests, to the linen-drapers or the bricklayers, while the demagogues " appeal to men as men." So in the French Revolution a crowd collected at every corner, to hear the expounding of a general idea. Only first principles, he concludes, can move large masses of humanity. " At the annunciation of principles, of ideas, the soul of man awakes and starts up, as an exile in a far distant land at the unexpected sounds of his native language." Now Coleridge was perfectly alive to the evils of intellectual abstraction. The devil, he remarked, "works precisely in the same way; he is a very clever fellow—I have no acquaintance with him, but I respect his evident talents." But by a *principle* he meant something rooted in religion or morals, and the distinction he had in mind is shown by his attack on the Utilitarians. Expediency might be a lower part of morals, a useful empirical guide in the prudential sphere of politics, but never could it supersede the inner light, which formed man at his beginning and pointed his goal—" which hath elsewhere its setting and cometh from afar."

Throughout his thought—however clouded and inconclusive—he has at least the supreme merit of clinging to the idea in things ; and " by an idea, I mean that conception of a thing which is given by the knowledge of its ultimate aim." To impart this measure of reality to the patchwork institutions of England, this was to be his work. As a Christian and a mystic, he believed that there was proceeding in the natural order a " redemptive process," a saving of the people by faith. The fixed principles of life are heaven-ordained, and national revival is the sacramental renewal by a nation of its obligations to the Highest. This mystic view, which explains some of Coleridge's radicalism, involves also the secondary importance he attached to mere political arrangement. He said in 1832, that he had " no faith in act of Parliament reform " ; " let us become a better people," ends the lay sermon of 1817, and then all these things will be added to us. The human soul is his real interest ; all progress, he thought, had been made by minorities ; " the lonely walks of uninterested theorists " had changed the face of the world. Of all sweeping or mechanical measures he was sceptical, and gives a far higher place to the nearer moralities of home, friendship, and country. " Let us beware of that proud philosophy, which affects to inculcate philanthropy, while it denounces every home-born feeling by which it is produced and nurtured." The finest flowers of civilization have grown " in a circle defined by human affections, the first firm sod within which becomes sacred beneath the quickened step of the returning citizen." The glory of Greece perished with her independence, and " in order to be men we must be patriots."

His attitude towards the State, in the sense of an organized governmental unit, is nearer, then, to that of the early fathers of the Church than to the intensely civic view of Rousseau or of Burke. Religion was, for him, " the centre of gravity " ; not Christianity necessarily, for that was only " a blessed accident, a providential boon," but rather all those forces which distinguish man from the brute and make a people a spiritual body.

" To preserve the stores and to guard the treasures of past civilization, and thus to bind the present with the past ; to perfect and add to the same, and thus to connect the present with the future ; but especially to diffuse through the whole community and to every native entitled to its laws and rights that quantity and quality of knowledge, which was indispensable both for the understanding of those rights and for the performance of those duties correspondent," here are the functions of that higher division, those Levites of the nation, whom he calls " the National Church." He went even further, and declared the Church to be " in idea, the only pure democracy," for she alone looks to essential merit, and not to the external accidents and compromises of birth, class, or property—she only can accept men as really equal. On this view the State is almost non-moral ; its internal arrangements are merely material for prudence which, though a department of morals, is an inferior and a subaltern. Political liberty is thus not in itself an end ; " though desirable, even for its own sake, it yet derived its main value as the means of calling forth and securing other advantages and excellencies, the activities of industry, the security of life and property, the peaceful energies of genius and manifold talent, the development of the moral virtues."

In our own day the noontide heat and radiance of the State has passed its height. The stars of other systems of political obligations are re-appearing, and the claims of groups, guilds and Churches, begin to compete with the legal or the metaphysical notion of State sovereignty. For this reason alone Coleridge's thought will probably win an increasing audience but, that apart, it deserves considera-tion as an eloquent reminder from a conservative of genius, that behind the State's façade lie a number of older and more spiritual allegiances.

His positive view of the State is not logically convinc-ing, but a mass of broken and scattered ideas, many of which show an unexpected worldly wisdom. As a moralist, he will naturally have nothing to do with " the bestial theory " of Hobbes, or those who build society on force and fear : " if there be any difference between a government and a band of robbers, an act of consent must be supposed on the part of the people governed." And his interpretation of such " consent " marks his modernity. Society began, he reasons, with the very creation of man, a creature endowed with conscience, and with the distinction of right and wrong. " A still-beginning, never-ceasing force of moral cohesion," " an ever-originating contract "—this, and no immutable code, is the real and self-renewing font of political obligation. The moral atoms impelled by this cohesion are essentially free agents, must therefore have a free sphere of action, and this is furnished by property. And where property exists, " there must be inequality of property ; the nature of the earth and the nature of the mind unite to make the contrary impossible." For protection of property, men superimposed a particular political structure upon the original social bond, and to defend property, life, religion, and personal freedom, are the negative ends of the State. Not that its duties end here, nor is its warfare ever accomplished ; since " with states, as well as individuals, not to be progressive is to be retrograde." The natural instincts implanted by the Creator demand satisfaction, and the State has accordingly three positive duties ; " to make the means of subsistence more easy to each individual ; to secure to each of its members the hope of bettering his own condition, or that of his children ; the development of those faculties which are essential to his humanity—that is, to his rational and

moral being." All this involves the further duty of
State education, with its important corollary—"the
discouragement of all such tenures and relations,
as must in the very nature of things render this knowledge inert, and cause the good seed to perish as it
falls."

Coleridge was too abstract a brain not to think that
" few are the minds that really govern," and " the neces-
sary ignorance of the numerical majority," their preoccu-
pation with " some one feeling or view " and not with
comprehensive truth, was one of his stock arguments
against sweeping reform. He believed, moreover, with
all sincerity, in function as the rule of life, finding in
theology and natural science alike the proof of an ascending scale in creation. But he would give most weight to
the argument that real unity is only to be found in an
equilibrium of opposing elements ; politically, then,
" there is no unity for a people, but in a representation of
national interests—a delegation from the passions or
wishes of the individuals themselves is a rope of sand."
Democracy might flow as the arterial blood of the
commonwealth, but must not usurp the place of the
limbs ; the notion of the State rests upon aristocracy,
classes, interests, and property, which give outward
scope to the provision of nature. It remains, however,
true that there are paths, which in time would lead to
democracy, implicit in his sketch of the State's duties to
its citizens—contingent and potential new roads, as it
were, which are cut out of his ruling principles. It is
part of his greatness that these principles are so expanding
and not closed, that the trees along his avenues have

within them this sap, and spring, and promise of new leaf.

The State, then, is " a body politic having the principle of its unity within itself," and turning upon " equipoise and interdependency." The *lex equilibrii* is the constitution. This is so, not merely in hard fact ; for the constitution, as in bodies natural, expresses not only what has been actually evolved from, but likewise whatever is potentially contained in, the seminal principle of the particular " body." We can, then, speak of the " idea " of our constitution as existing, altogether apart from the ebbings and flowings of our constitutional history ; like life itself, it has reality, and in our own State, as in all, room must be found for the two rival interests of permanence and progression. The first rests on the land, and all its connected life ; the second is represented by the professional, mercantile, and distributing classes. On a just balance between permanence and progression the State's prosperity depends. So, for instance, highly as he valued a good agricultural system, he put down the collapse of unreformed England to the unfair predominance in the legislature of the landed interest. But, even when well maintained, this balance between landed and mercantile proprietors will not suffice to the health of the nation. " The organized powers brought within containing channels," which property represents, must be kept in proportion to the " free and permeative life and energy of the nation." Political power conceded to energy and intellect is dangerous without rooting those faculties in property, which ensures " at least a strong probability " of moral fibre. Equally disastrous is the

partisan exclusion of those economically fitted for the
suffrage ; so are any laws or customs which impede free
circulation of property, or tie up wealth in " abiding
masses."

The poet's views upon property, much used in parts
by the anti-capitalist writers who followed him, embody
in all their sentiment at least one kernel of still relevant
truth. He was not, after the Peace of Amiens at any rate,
a Socialist, and denounced the offence to morals involved
in schemes of confiscation. He repudiated, too, the
fancy that the State had national possessions which it
could resume, as one of those " half-truths, the most
dangerous of errors (as those of the poor visionaries called
Spenceans)." But he held constantly that property in
land was in historical origin a trust, expressly charged
with duties to the community, and he found the root of
the peasants' misery after the war in the introduction of
the commercial spirit into the properly moral relation of
landlord and tenant. As for any practicable test of State
control over private property, he made the far-reaching
suggestion that the State could invalidate any trespass
upon " its own inalienable and untransferable property—
I mean the health, strength, honesty, and filial love of its
children."

The last of these conditions, which constitute the
well-balanced state, is not the least fruitful or sapient.
There must be a due proportion between the actual and
the potential political machinery ; between, let us say,
Parliament and people. An extreme democracy, Coleridge argued, left nothing in reserve ; " the whole will
of the body politic is in act at every moment."· But in

England, "with all her venerable heirlooms, and with all her germs of reversionary wealth," the nation has not delegated its all—it keeps back a latent, "a yet auguster thing." Its manifestations no man can predict, but there come "epochs of growth and reparation," which make "audible to the historian that voice of the people, which is the voice of God." The wise State, the poet implies, will keep its ear close to the ground.

"The door of the Cabinet," said Coleridge, "has a quality the most opposite to the ivory gate of Virgil ; it suffers no dreams to pass through it." Some of the political thought here examined may seem to be but visions, caught up by the banks of Alph the sacred river, "meandering in mazy motion" down to "caverns measureless to man." But much the greater part would appear to have a permanent value, precisely because it is filled with the moral passion which transcends the prejudices of one generation, or the feelings of one class. Coleridge was not, like the philosophic Radical, concerned only to save the men of to-day from dead yesterday, or like the lesser tribe that copied Burke, to defend to-day against the clamant future. He had at heart divinely-ordained truths for men of all and any time—obedience to which would ensure even earthly felicity. He predicted that by going back to the reality, the idea, in ancient institutions, they might yet be made to serve a new age. Of all and every class and fabric he asked, what is its moral purpose—what is its place in the celestial plan ? Putting it at the lowest, he remonstrated against the anarchists of the intellect, that some things in a great society must be fixed and unquestionable ; against the reactionaries, that even these fixed truths were not stationary pillars, but living seeds ; he argued that not only progress, but permanence also, was best safeguarded by allowing the development of a nation's mind. Somewhere he gives his definition of the purest patriots ; " accustomed to regard all the affairs of man as a process, they never hurry and they never pause."

H

NEWMAN

NEWMAN

TO the future historical student of the early twentieth century few things will appear so surprising as the attitude of the Anglican Church towards the General Strike of 1926. Stripping the question of the confusion introduced by the coal controversy, he will find that a number of those then leading that Church invited the Government of an ultra-democratic country to surrender to physical force a position from which neither votes nor reasoning process had dislodged them, and equated that elected Government for purposes of negotiation with a section of its subjects. On the vital point of the continued authority of Parliamentary government he will find that in this year the Church of Elizabeth and Laud, indirectly at the least, supported those who challenged the full authority of Parliament, and he will seek the point of its departure from its traditional position. Such an investigation would begin with the great name of Newman, the most living force in the making of modern Anglo-Catholicism.

None, except those who reason from the Sermon on the Mount to Blue-books, will ask from a Church or churchmen a detailed exposition of the State, of political rights and social obligation, and Newman's works contain no such applied creed. Beginning in his Calvinist youth with those " two, and two only, supreme and luminously self-evident beings, myself and my Creator," he came, indeed, to an immeasurably wider view of humanity, but to the end he set out from theological tenets and separated the province of the Church from the world. He never thought peace the primary duty of the priest, nor to civilize the first function of the Church. She had her revelation, which completed and sanctified natural religion ; her mission did not extend to dictate particulars of civil governance, and could not be summarized in "tavern toasts." Only indirectly, then, has the Cardinal's thought affected English politics ; yet the rich stream irrigates fields and villages far from its local channel, and the whole principle of authority in the nineteenth century would be unintelligible without reference to the Oxford movement.

The scanty secular thinkers to whom he admitted his obligation were Wordsworth, Southey, Scott, and Cole- ridge, and politically he stands on the flank of the romantic reaction. All that made life significant he found wrapped up in dogma ; all that he thought evil, in Liberalism. " To prefer intellectual excellence to moral," " opposition for its own sake, striving against the truth, because it happens to be commanded us "—thus he defined the enemy, that unbridled goddess Reason, crowned by revolution. Humanly, he felt himself part of an older England. He continued to speak in old age, like Gladstone, of " the gentry," in a meaning now extin- guished, and doubted, with Maine and Bagehot, whether the social frame could bear the shock of the Reform Bill

of 1867. Unmistakable consciousness of aristocracy sits
on the brow of him whose thought was pointed by daily
contact with Hurrell Froude, that " high Tory of the
Cavalier stamp." He opposed Peel on Emancipation,
and deplored the French Revolution of 1830. Like the
young Gladstone, he discerned " a certain element of
anti-Christ " in the Reform Bill, and only habitual reading
discovers that when Newman speaks of " George the
Good," he means the third Hanoverian. But a wide gulf
puts him apart from the mere stationary enemies of
reform, for " to be stationary is to lose ground, and to
repose is to fail."

Principle, even the principle of authority, has life
within it, and leads its followers by paths that trespass
from the high road of present convention. " Tory as I
still am, theoretically and historically," Newman wrote
after his memorable return from abroad in 1833, " I
begin to be a Radical practically." Divine right,
Cavaliers, and non-jurors had so far led him on, but the
times were changed, the aristocracy had apostatized,
the Church must rest on older and broader foundations.
Through a seventeenth century glass he had caught sight
of the seat of authority, on distant hills ; soon the glass
was discarded, union with the State dismissed as a mirage,
and the whole content and sanction of truth seen face to
face in a universal Church. To free themselves from
shams and phrases, to become humdrum for truth's
sake, to purge away dross from the English Tyre, had
become his and Froude's passion when they fell out with
the safe men, the conservatives of 1833, and this fierce
realism is an unchanging note in his teaching. " We

must take things as we find them "—this is the unceasing refrain of this Calvinist seeking Catholicity, and first among such verities was the depravity of man.

Viewing life as a whole, and the ocean of folly, crime, and unhappiness, on which man is cast away, he could conclude only either that God was not, or that man was alienated from Him by sin. The Fall is fundamental to him. A state of nature is barbarism ; man is naturally rebel, armed against truth with the " all corroding, all dissolving," fangs of intellect. There is, then, a maximum advance to any purely secular civilization ; there is such a thing as evil in the world—evil as a constant and militant energy. Not Christ, but Rousseau, predicted man's earthly perfectibility, and evil is not made good in becoming triumphant. " To speak as if what has been, and is, ought to be," is to make terms with Satan. The march of mind, progress so called, may be an advance into evil. " The usurpation of an invader, and the development (as it is called) of the popular power, are alike facts, and alike sins, in the sight of Him who forbids us to oppose constituted authority." " The false cheerfulness and the ill-founded hope and the blind charitableness " which refuse to face facts are broken reeds with the first stroke of calamity, and their exponents are branded with the curse falling on those who heal the people slightly, " crying ' Peace, peace,' when there is no peace."

When, therefore, the Anglican Newman of 1840 deplores " these wretched Socialists," or the Catholic of 1874 declares " no one can dislike the democratic principle more than I do," he is not speaking the language of the Carlton Club. Admitting, with his invincible

realism, it must needs be that the intellect, once a general
level of cultivation was reached, should fly off at multi-
tudinous tangents, he still refused to agree that the
humanly inevitable was thereby divinely right. The
future might settle " some way of uniting what is free
in the new structure of society with what is authoritative
in the old " ; but it was not the Church's business to
accommodate revealed truth to temporary emergency.

What, then, must be the sanction of the Christian
citizen's duty ? It lay in an original gift of nature, in
conscience, " the aboriginal Vicar of Christ." Conscience
is not self-will, or a right of doing as you please ; it is
the voice of God. Nor ordinarily is man left to discover
that voice by his private judgment ; both Church and
State are ordinances of God, each with its assigned, and
rarely conflicting, spheres of authority. Save in extraordinary cases, the Church's teaching of obedience is
unvarying and determined ; yes, obedience even to an
erroneous rule, even to " an insolent and aggressive
faction." For Christianity sanctions the political system ;
" I would have you recollect that the civil power is a
divine ordinance." It claims, too, " the allegiance of its
subjects on the ground of the tangible benefits of which
it is the instrument towards them " ; in the Sovereign is
" centred the order, the security, the happiness of a great
people." And if the State, under God's ordinance, ensures such blessings, " surely a man has to think twice,
and ought to be quite sure what he is doing, and to have
a clear case to produce in his behalf, before he sets up
any rival society to embarrass and endanger it." Reverence for law, he claims, wrecked the Chartist upheaval,

and no society could endorse the logical conclusions of Mill's *Liberty*.

" The indestructibility of good principle " was a favourite, indeed an inevitable, doctrine of the Cardinal. He gloried in being an Aristotelian, and found in Scripture what the master had taught, that Providence creates nothing in vain. Always advising against impatience, he asked men to study humanity on big maps, and to wait for the crumbling of evil. Liberalism was " too cold a principle to prevail," for life was made up of " order and warmth." As for the philosophy of utility, " it aimed low, but it has fulfilled its aim " ; comfort and materialism are all around us, but the greatest happiness does not yet seem to appeal to the greatest number. But " Toryism, that is, loyalty to persons, springs immortal in the human breast," and " religion is a spiritual loyalty."

A parallel with Disraeli, so marked in the last quoted surprising sentence, is neither irreverent nor fortuitous. In his own field each found mere conservatism entirely unsatisfying as a permanent and vital defence of authority, and searched in the human heart for springs of action more venerable than Protestantism, or Peel, or the police force. Newman, for purposes of controversy, himself drew the parallel here made. That religion should be the basis of society, he wrote in 1874, " all this was called Toryism and men gloried in the name—now it is called Popery, and reviled." Whatever the religious element in Disraeli's thought, whatever the relation between Hughenden, Rome, and Jerusalem, it will at least be recognized that in the permanent essence of a teaching, which is successfully to defend authority, there must be

something, in the widest sense, catholic ; universality,
the touchstone of Roman and medieval thinking, was the
prescription of Newman in the Church, as of Disraeli in
the State. *Securus judicat orbis terrarum.* This is the
sentence, " the shadow of a hand on the wall," which in
1839 struck dumb the Anglican defensive.

Here is the carefully-guarded test at which the wan-
derer at last arrived ; " the deliberate judgment, in which
the whole Church at length rests and acquiesces, is an
infallible prescription." It is the very rule which
Hooker and Burke made a canon of conservative thinking,
and in light of which Newman is their spiritual child. It
fixes the *depositum fidei* in no rigid, changeless code, but
depicts it rather as the permanent frame of a great
building, in which many generations are to live, adapting,
improving, retracing. The Church of the first four
centuries, like the Whigs of 1789, might speak with
divided voice ; Newman fell back, as Burke in like case,
upon this concept of a living great society. Our ancestors'
wisdom, said Newman in 1829, in part divinely revealed
truths, in part nature's lessons, were transmitted through
men " many of whom cannot enter into them, or receive
them themselves—still on, on, from age to age, not the less
truths because many of the generations through which
they are transmitted are unable to prove them." Such
faith might be shamed by " the argument of an hour,"
and " any Cambridge man " could refute Keble ; but
the stream still flowed, and the " notes " of the Church, its
distinction from heresy, are found in life, in fruitfulness,
in " continued and abiding energy." Truth, that is,
admits of, and claims, development ; as for untruth, " its

formulæ end in themselves, without development, because they are words—they are barren, because they are dead."

This plastic notion of development, of the related complexity of things past and present and to come, is what chiefly lends permanence to Newman's ideas, and makes him, perforce, a political teacher. For he who, like Newman or Burke, submits the dogma of the hour to the long judgment of time will make allowance for the actual working of things, even of a concept so severe as infallibility. He refuses to destroy an institution or body of teaching, on the whole beneficent, by tearing apart its connected strands ; he sees general advance in spite of partial retreat—the steady flood tide, in spite of the tired waves vainly breaking. Newman, it is true, had a full share of that scepticism which forms an invariable element in authoritative thought ; scepticism, that is, of the unaided reason, and of facile chatter about progress. He held that man's intrinsic nature did not change greatly from century to century, and found no infallible medicine in forms of government.

He argued, rather, that there were tangible realities— God and nature, good and evil—on which rested the living, lasting systems of law and theology, which outlived and transcended individual Popes and parliaments. Yet natural religion and revelation, which began, did not exhaust the Divine purpose. They furnish, as it were, the raw material of truth, but beyond lie the infinite possibilities to be made of these fixed minima by human capacity. He did not find that informed opinion was won by a wholly intellectual process, by what is termed "reason," as opposed to faith; rather, that men act every

day upon the strength of assumptions which, though
non-demonstrable, are still sovereign. Probability must
enter into all decision, and we who largely take God upon
trust must trust too the instincts He has given us. " Life
is for action. If we insist on proofs for everything, we
shall never come to action ; to act you must assume, and
that assumption is faith." And this full assent will be
at its clearest when nearest to the concrete—nearest, in
especial, to persons, who are the realities most intensely
grasped. Men may, indeed, arrive at truth by very different mixtures of all the elements of assent, but they must
begin, and will most safely end, with the original forces
common to us all. Toryism, seen as adherence to persons
—conscience, as a personal command to follow a supreme
and personal Will—in this most personal sense Newman
grounded the indestructibility of principle. He seems to
end, then, with God and the individual soul, those two
" luminous " realities with which his religious life began,
and finds the proper field of the Church in raising the
individual to moral victory.

No distinction (save that given by certain dates) has
here been made between the views of Newman the
Anglican and of the Roman cardinal, upon the relation of
the Church to society, for no break is apparent in his
social teaching. Never ceasing to make religion the
primary end of man, he never seems to have thought that
anything but religion was the province of the Church.
When religious truth was threatened by society, he would
resist ; but he did not view the Church's Kingdom as of
this world. His application of Scripture was the reverse
of that of the Puritan : beyond an immutable body of

truth, he found a wide sphere left for the working of reason and experience. He never declares that one species only of government or one form of property is agreeable to Christian teaching ; rather he seems to subject all species and forms to certain binding principles. The authority which in matters doctrinal he found in a living Church, in things of this world he appears to place in the accumulative age, wisdom, and rationality, represented by an old civilization and a legal order. He held that religion, though it transcended, did not supersede the order established by the original endowments of man, and continued the Catholic teaching of the moral guilt incurred by those who take the sword to accelerate the operation of law.

BULWER LYTTON

BULWER LYTTON

MOST of the members of Lord Derby's three Ministries, with the outstanding exception of Disraeli, do not easily engrave themselves on the memory ; for the greater part, like Carlyle's Merovingian kings, they have jolted on in their ox-wagons into the eternal silences. But one of his numerous Secretaries of State for the Colonies is a familiar name in another connexion, as the author of those almost endless novels that deal with things ending or in declension, *The Last of the Barons*, *The Last Days of Pompeii*, and *Harold, the Last of the Saxon Kings*.

Bulwer Lytton was not, for reasons soon to be seen, a normal politician, but he illustrates, for all that, at least one of the fundamentals of our politics. It is on the margin that the economist isolates his data and draws his conclusions, and it is on the broad meandering margin between the two historic parties that the historian of party finds the germ of future development. Observation of its occupants at decisive epochs—of the " country " party under William III, of the Hanoverian Tories, of the Burke Whigs, or of the Peelites—impresses upon him the conviction of an ever-repeated process, of a steady flow away from the left of politics towards the right. Making every allowance for personal or ephemeral circumstance—that is, for perhaps half the battle—it can still hardly be accident that Harley and Bolingbroke were of Whig descent, that the Pitts and Burke were the same, that Derby was a Whig convert, that Disraeli and Chamberlain began as radical reformers. If, proceeding further, the historian eliminates the case of the leaders as exceptional, and applies his tentative conclusion to the rank and file, he reaches at last a physical law, a law of diminishing returns—the stolid fact that young men are radical and elderly men conservative. Conservatism, on this reasoning, withstands the buffetings of time and tide just because it never ceases to receive accretions from the liberalism of the past.

The application of this law, ever adjusted to countless variations of individual character, is long suspended, though not invalidated, in the case of genius, and the story of Lytton's life amply explains the devious route by which he ultimately reached the obvious end. The child of a wretched marriage, he was badly brought up, repressed when he asked for freedom, and spoiled when he needed discipline. He was thus allowed to decide for himself that he was too mature for a public school, and to leave one Cambridge college, where he would have been kept in order, for another where he ordered himself. A little more routine would have shaken off that obsession of self-identity. " I am too impatient of subordination," he wrote in middle life, " an immense fault in the acting man," and his own most miserable marriage was wrecked on this same unwholesome self-consciousness. The weakness of his novels, with all their surpassing narrative gift, seems to derive from the same

source ; the " want of soundness, manliness, and simplicity of mind," noted by Macaulay, goes deeper than
style. His heroes, of all ages and nations, come from
one and the same patrician Bohemia ; draped in togas or
clamped in chain of mail, they all writhe, sob, and posture,
as though they were contemporaries of Byron and eking
out a penance on soda-water. The audiences of Lytton's
speeches were very various—Edinburgh students, Leeds
mechanics, or private soldiers—but they usually heard a
good deal of the old strain ; he could hardly speak of
war without Mars, or of Russia without Scythian hordes,
and his oratory at its worst bears a painful resemblance
to the after-dinner speeches at the cricket festival of
Dingley Dell.

A Bohemian dislike for " respectability " breathes
through his political writing. The English, he thought,
had a weakness for pushing common sense into stodgi-
ness, and for " elevating apathy into virtue." " If a
gentleman walked betimes in the park with his seven
children and a very ugly wife, the regularity of such
conduct would have stamped him as an unexceptionable
politician." He cordially disliked what may be called
the " no nonsense " school ; " they write upon their
minds the motto ' no cant,' and what they do not compre-
hend they believe to be insincere." All this came
naturally from one who was himself the last of the dandies.
In their vital, tired, underworld he with Lady Blessington,
Mrs. Norton, and Louis Napoleon shook down the
blossoms of love, letters and politics, as though in an
airless conservatory ; for a day or so he had worn the
ring which once was Byron's, and which now adorned

successive admirers of Lady Caroline Lamb. He liked
then, as in old age, to dabble with the occult, with the
later Platonists, American table rappers, and the Rosi-
crucian fraternity. Let us remember, too, that he forms
one angle in Disraeli's triangular compliment—that he
had not known conceit like Charles Greville's, " though
I have read Cicero and was intimate with Lytton Bulwer."

Curious material, we might say, for a Cabinet Minister,
even in the age of Palmerston. But mind and body have
a complexity of relation outside the text-books, and the
strange gods and goddesses at whose shrines great men—
even Nelson himself—have worshipped, leave intact their
life of service. In spite, then, of all morbidity, in spite
of what Derby called his " pathological " letters, the core
of Lytton was that of a man of action. Fifty-nine items in
his bibliography prove his enormous toil and his native
endowments. If his historical novels are not, as a whole,
the best in the language, it is hard to think of any that
are better. *My Novel* and *Kenelm Chillingley* draw mid-
Victorian England with the hand of a master. *England
and the English*, *St. Stephen's*, *Money*, and *The Lady of
Lyons* are satire, political verse, and drama, if not of the
first, then at the top of the second order of merit. He
was in the front rank of House of Commons speakers
when speeches still deflected policy, and as a Cabinet
Minister won the good opinion of Gladstone. Stripped
of all flummery, his was a massive and a realist mind, a
type of the landed commoners he sprang from, fired and
strung up by intense pride of race. His literary taste
was masculine, and it was authors who were " broadly
English " whom he commended as models to his son.

A streak of Blougram tempered his thickcoming imagination ; " Browning's bishop was right in his way, but what he says as a cynic I say as a gentleman and an artist."

One strong impression he must leave upon anyone who is at pains to read him at large ; that is, a rightness of judgment which sometimes climbs to predictive power. A letter of 1834 to Disraeli from Ireland does not leave much more to be said. " Sooner or later, this must end in a despotism or a republic. Perhaps both. The Orangemen are the true link between English Government and the Irish, and yet that link *must* be broken." His marmoreal sentences upon his contemporaries have sometimes become part of our political fabric, and we know, without thinking of the author, who was " the Rupert of debate," and how " languid Johnny glowed to glorious John." He had said of Peel in 1836, " if I were a Tory I should consider him my worst enemy," and followed it up, in *St. Stephen's*, with a famous summary on " the man at once most timid and most bold." Living as a young man in the age of Croker and Jeffrey, he welcomed the new school of power whom they had cudgelled. Coleridge, he held, was " by far the largest mind of his age "—" wherever the leviathan moves either his head or his tail, there is a stir in the ocean felt miles and leagues off." Again, " no writer more unvulgarizes the mind " than Wordsworth, whose " refined and refining Toryism" he laid bare. Johnson, to give a last instance, is in a class above Macaulay, for " he says finer things in a finer way."

In politics, like Halifax the trimmer, he was one of

those with whom posterity usually agrees. Twenty years before the stamp duties vanished, he had championed an untaxed Press. He urged universal education long before 1870, adult schools half a century before University extension, and no class feeling ever buried in him a ruling instinct that a broad highway for the talents was the path of safety for old institutions. He supported Parliamentary reform against the Tories, a distinction between inherited and precarious incomes against Gladstone, the Factory Acts against Cobden. The nation's honour set up a vibration in him which party considerations could not silence ; he attacked with the same ardour Russell's Foreign Enlistment Bill and Palmerston's inglorious heroics over China.

A once famous speech of 1859 against further enlargement of the franchise, though now belied by later history, is well worth putting alongside some things in Bagehot, and more than worth a good many gloomy pages of Carlyle and Sir Henry Maine. " One moment more to this Bill. It is said not to be final. No Reform Bill can be. The fault you allege is its merit. It is its merit, if it meets one of the requirements of the day present, and does not give to-day what you may regret to-morrow that you cannot restore. Democracy is like the grave—it perpetually cries, ' give, give,' and, like the grave, it never returns what it has once taken. But you live under a constitutional monarchy, which has all the vigour of health, all the energy of movement. Do not surrender to democracy that which is not yet ripe for the grave."

Lytton was elected to the Parliament of 1831 as a reformer, and as a reformer, even a Radical, but never a

Whig, he continued. Godwin, Ebenezer Elliott, and the Mills watched his career with friendly eyes, and the one member of Grey's ministry with whom he found himself in accord was the Radical Durham. At one moment he was dazzled by that recurring mirage of progressive Conservatives, the hope of a new national party, but the typical Whig scheme always suffocated him. *England and the English*, published in 1833, tilted against their patronizing philosophy and their discriminating patronage. " What son, what brother, what nephew, what cousin, what remote and unconjectured relative in the Genesis of the Greys has not fastened his limpet to the rock of the national expenditure ? "

Twenty years after, he traced the public anger at the scandals of the Crimea to this same " Celestial empire." " In the composition of your Cabinets you have, one after another, installed a combination of families and privileged houses like a sacred caste, and have contrived to sour, to chill, and to alienate the energy, the intellect, the enthusiasm of that class of your supporters in whom the people can recognise their own hardy children." All know, he continues, the secret of Whig management ; " it consists in saying to the Radicals, ' Support us, or you will let in those horrible Tories,' and in whispering to the Conservatives, ' Bear with us, or those horrible Radicals will upset the country '."

On the other hand, for Radicalism as it emerged after 1848 and moved away from the teaching of his friend Mill, he had no liking. He honoured freedom of opinion, but disbelieved in the massed " march of mind," for he thought individual excellence to be the making of the

State and a heroic type the end of education. More particularly did he disdain the teaching of the Manchester school, partly as pure evil, partly as sheer illusion. " A Republic is cheap," he told his Liberal friend Forster in 1848, " but if ever that hour arrives it shall not be, if I and a few like me live, a republic of millers and cotton-spinner, but either a republic of gentlemen or a republic of workmen—either is better than those wretched money spiders who would sell England for 1s. 6d."

His social outlook was thus much like that of the well-born republicans of the seventeenth century, who had opposed alike a King, a priesthood, and a mob. The people, he declared, were not a class ; " gentlemen," an aristocracy (a word to which he gave its original meaning), were the true representatives of a nation. Observe the speech with which he prepared to defend, against his own party, Gladstone's repeal of the paper duties, and its tone towards the Lords.

> " If this House were to accept certain doctrines, which I never thought I should live to hear from English lips— doctrines that would make the House of Lords the habitual and regular partner with us in the taxation of our constituents— if this House could so betray the memory of our ancestors and the heritage of our children, I know not how one well-born gentleman of spirit and honour would condescend to accept a seat in it."

And with it compare a letter of ten years before :— " Show me a class of gentlemen, an aristocracy in short, and I will form a conjecture as to the duration of any free constitution ; without that, between Crown, soldiers, traders, and mobs, I am all at sea."

Any man holding such views must have been increasingly ill at ease among the Whig-Liberal majority that controlled politics between the fall of Peel and the death of Palmerston, but in point of fact Lytton had earlier severed himself from most Whigs over one burning question. For while they as a party proposed henceforward to ground their economic system upon freedom of imports, Lytton clung to the scheme which Canning had bequeathed and which Peel had once found sufficient, of reform coupled with a measure of protection. From the first he argued that this question was one of those with which " political economy, mere mercantile loss and gain, has least to do." The real stakes were " high social considerations " ; and the real consequences " lie in the next age."

" The question then to be decided is whether by altering the proportionate labour of the population, whether by augmenting yet more, not the prosperity of commerce and manufactures alone, but the masses of men employed on them, you have not altered for the worse the staple character and spirit of the people."

This was written in 1846, the year of Peel's great revolution ; five years before, Lytton had lost his seat upon this very issue, and the Whigs had shown no zeal meantime to provide him with another.

It was not till 1852 that he re-entered Parliament, this time as a supporter of Lord Derby. He had heralded his change of allegiance with a statement of protectionist faith, in his *Letters to John Bull*. There he advocated protection as a measure of conciliation, to save the agricultural interest which one party had ignored and the other abandoned, suggesting that a low fixed duty could be justified on grounds of humanity, to tide over the present generation of farmers. He asked why the principle of taxation for revenue, still sanctioned in the case of many petty commodities, should not be extended to the capital case of corn. If duties on foreign silk were defended " not only as sources of revenue, but as some aid against foreign competition . . . why deprive yourselves of a source of revenue larger than is derived from all these duties put together, because it would aid, during a fearful strain upon its energies, a class that comprises at least a fourth of your population ? " He deplored the overwhelming political predominance which free imports must assure to our industrial cities, " where the spirit of an eternal election agitates the mass of the everlasting crowd." Once more he lamented that economists took no heed of " living men, their passions, and habits, and prejudices," and predicted that starvation wages in agriculture would follow on a crash in the profits of farming. Observing that the nations which paid most lip service to the laws of Nature still retained the highest tariffs, he blew out of the water the moral delusion, or perhaps the cant, of free trade all round. Some day, he prophesied, distress in the English countryside would teach the English manufacturer that the home market was worth preserving.

But not on this question only did he dissent from victorious Liberalism, which, he felt, was imperilling the quality of our race. Power " must be intellectual, or it has no duration," and the mere representation of numbers must end in the disfranchisement of energy and brain.

"Once Americanize the House of Commons" (an understatement, he argued, since the American Senate saves Congress from its worst mistakes), "and you would lose more in the intellectual attributes that create your real power than you could obtain by all the popular vigour you could get through manhood suffrage and electoral districts."

A franchise, in the abstract, had no more claim to be called a natural right than any other social expedient, and the monopoly of power by one class must jeopardize the commonwealth, "which can only be fairly represented where the middle class is, on the whole, largely preponderant." If Liberalism of this urban ballot-box type insisted on its pound of flesh, he foresaw the coming of "an Avenger who, uniting popular attributes with an anti-liberal philosophy, would seek to destroy all that is now understood by the enlightened name of Liberal." Always he reasoned that "the thoughtful essence of the life of nations, the tranquil people," were benefited rather by good administration than by loud-sounding reform—a benefit, by 1851, he was persuaded, that would come most surely from the new Conservatism of his old friend Disraeli.

The conception of what Lytton meant by Conservatism is best revealed by a fragmentary essay, dated by his son as of about 1852. Its *rôle*, he there says, is to conserve the organic principles peculiar to our country. Its object must be "duration," its bane is disorganization, and in the last resort social order outweighs even political liberty. The first organic principle of England was aristocracy, in the fullest sense of that abused term.

" What Conservatism aims at is not the maintenance of nobility, except so far as nobility forms an element in the grander organization of aristocracy ; it aims at preserving the general influence, both on laws and on society, of the chief man or the best, whether in character, intelligence, property, or birth—taking property as one of the guarantees, but only as one, that give to a citizen a stake in the welfare of his country and the preservation of order."

It is no part of Conservative policy to buttress the peerage by exterior privilege ; " if Conservatism were to seek by direct laws to strengthen the outward power of aristocracy, it would instantly defeat its own object." Far other is his own idea :

" To elevate the masses, in character and feeling, to that standard which Conservatism seeks in aristocracy—in other words, to aristocratize the community, so that the greatest liberty to the greatest number might not be the brief and hazardous effect of a sudden revolutionary law, but the gradual result of that intellectual power to which liberty is indispensable."

To preserve the ancient framework of the State, but to renew it perpetually on its journey through time, by admitting any found worthy to inherit it—such, says Lytton, is the policy of an enduring people, who advance hardily but with caution by parallels from their old defences.

His political career was an episode in the life of a man of letters, and probably no one but Disraeli could have put him in the Cabinet. One must doubt whether it was only increasing deafness which stopped Derby including him again in 1866, when the Tories returned for another whiff of office. He was offered (and declined) the throne of Greece, but not again the Secretaryship for the Colonies. Yet this interlude of the novelist as party politician has its interest, if only as suggesting that party considered as an object in itself is hardly worth the lifelong application of an intelligent being. It is possible that this reflection might reconcile Lytton, could he see England now, to the fulfilment of many things which he foresaw and detested. His candid friends, Derby and Disraeli, took that leap in the dark over the second Reform Bill which began the process of electoral illumination. The cities have devoured his England of villages, squires, and parsons. Centralization has undermined, as he feared, some local vitality, even in dispelling chaos. On the other hand, universal education, diffused by agencies he had not dreamed of, has in a sense realized his hope of " aristocratizing " democracy.

Here, at any rate, was one whose life was largely spent in protest against the ruling forces of the last century— against the identification of liberty with *laissez faire*, of money wealth with national profit, of theoretic right with social good. Few men have combined such ardour for positive reform with such passion for the permanent causes of land, hearth, and home, and the need for affection, which he owned to be the key to his stormy life, is also the heart of his political teaching. Could he return, he might retort upon modern civilization that politics would not be the worse for more such makers of fiction ; he might ask " Have not my dreams come true, and has not the Avenger arisen ? "

WALTER BAGEHOT

WALTER BAGEHOT

W ALTER BAGEHOT, author of *Lombard Street*,
The English Constitution, and *Physics and Politics*,
who was born on the 3rd of February, 1826, did
not desire fame with posterity, which he likened
to "a moth going into Chancery," but wished for
life.

But he died at fifty-one, leaving at least three books
still read, in all probability, more widely and continuously
by men of his race than those of any other Victorian.
This "man of genius, who being dead yet speaketh"
(so Dicey wrote in 1914), still speaks to the "stupid"
English, whose lack of brain he put so high in the scale
of civic virtues ; so great is his living power that it is
hard to believe he was born a hundred years ago when
Eldon was Chancellor—Eldon of whom he wrote later,
"it is the most difficult thing in the world to believe that
there was ever such a man."

Style is commonly taken to be the secret of literary
vitality, and Bagehot's may be deemed perfection for the
public discussion of great subjects. To talk with him was
compared to "riding a horse with a perfect mouth," and
all that makes writing delightful—ease, sympathy,
humour, nervous power—seems to come to Bagehot in his
stride. His chance words have won the sincerest flattery

from generations of schoolboys ; the Cabinet as a
" hyphen," " the cake of custom," the " dignified " parts
of our Government, have become (what he always detested) catchwords. Every page of his work has a living
phrase. " Toryism is enjoyment."   " The sacred tor-
pidity " of Oxford. Of Wordsworth, that Mr. Keble
" has translated him for women." Of a constitutional
statesman : " a man of common opinions and uncommon
abilities." " He who runs may read, but it does not seem
likely he will think." " The great difficulty which
history records is not that of the first step, but that of the
second step." Of Milton, that " he made God argue."

But bouquets like these do wrong to the depth and
richness of English earth in Bagehot. Reality, he always
declared, was the secret of excellence, and his books live
for the very reason that he was not a book-maker. He
both felt and reasoned ; his thought was implicit with
action, his action compressed thought. He lived so
intensely because he blended two gifts rarely conjoined ;
a mystic and conservative moral physique with a liberal
and defining intellect. If a star danced over his birth,
as for his favourites Scott and Shakespeare, it was a star
with reflection in it. It is more curious that it shone
over Stuckey's Bank at Langport, in Somerset, where this
genius was born and died. For his intellectual action had
throughout this matter-of-fact background. By birth a
Somerset squire, who till middle life hunted a pack of
harriers ; by immediate descent, son of a Unitarian
Whig and nephew of a country banker ; by education,
the product of London University, Bristol business, and
journalism ; by profession, always a banker and for

seventeen years editor of the *Economist*. As a Parliamentary candidate he was not in any sense successful. He could have been Finance Member in India ; characteristically, he declined because his duty as a son kept him at home.

He was, in short, a man of genius who led a very ordinary life, which, however, he found enough for wisdom and enjoyment. " At bottom, perhaps," he says of Cornewall Lewis, " he did not much object to be thought a little commonplace," and he himself clearly had some of Lincoln's partiality for the ordinary people and the ordinary duties of life. He looked upon them with an eye which some have thought cynical, but here his defence of Clough from the same charge may paint himself :

" He saw what it is considered cynical to see—the absurdities of many persons, the pomposities of many creeds, the splendid zeal with which missionaries rush on to teach what they do not know, the wonderful earnestness with which most incomplete solutions of the universe are thrust upon us as complete and satisfying."

His firm belief in government by discussion came from this same distrust of " yokes," intellectual or academic ; " we know at least," says his reasoning against despotism, " that facts are many ; that progress is complicated : that burning ideas (such as young men have) are mostly false and always incomplete." But his realism was never barren ; he insisted, rather, on giving every element in the human frame its full but its proper place. Admiring both freedom and order, he thought an " animated moderation " the best quality for public life. He did not care for sentimental impulse, which he found to govern men of rare genius like Shelley or Sterne, and condemned that " irritable intellect which sets an undue value on new theories of society and morality." Writing, he felt, should be logical and defined in form. Poetry should be " memorable and emphatic, intense and *soon over*." The pure simplicity he coveted he found most in Wordsworth, with that meditative calm which he never ceased to ask for both in books and men. He preferred, therefore, Hazlitt to Lamb, and considered the eighteenth century to be underated. Men so unlike as Bolingbroke and Gladstone alike lacked the tranquillity of the highest statesmanship, which, with a dash more of the animal and less of the vegetable, he would have discovered in Cornewall Lewis. But brain of some sort, Bagehot emphasized, must be the first condition of government. His cautious views on the franchise were coloured deeply by this fear of the half-educated ; " the intellectual poorness " of the Established Church appeared to him its greatest danger ; much though he admired Dickens' vitality, he found one damning blot— he did not think. More than once he dissected, in his almost surgical style, the mental shortcomings of the county members of Parliament ; " the long row of county members, so fresh and respectable-looking," " the finest brute votes in Europe."

For all that, he was too true a realist to be a " highbrow," and no man did more to demolish the reign of abstractions and sophistries. The " thin acuteness " of agnosticism left him cold, for a personal religion alone could warm the cravings of the human spirit. Admiring Mill, he was never a utilitarian, and in a famous essay on

the Edinburgh Reviewers smote the "polished liberalism," which had stoned the romantic prophets with its
" this will never do." At this his sword leaves the
scabbard : " both Mr. Wordsworth and Lord Jeffrey
have received their reward." From his youthful and
rather jaunty defence of Louis Napoleon down to the last
edition of his mature work on " the English Constitution," he persistently declined to view politics as an immutable branch of ethics. He found nothing so perfect
in the inevitable constitution of society as to warrant
wholesale application of idealist morals ; " if you will
only write a description of it, any form of government
will seem ridiculous." Reality was what he looked for,
and high in the circle of verities he placed the convictions
which he found in his own intellectual masters—in
Shakespeare, Wordsworth, Clough, or Newman : that
men are not the same but different, that reason is mixed
with body and soul, that good and evil are blent in all
the operations of Nature, and that words, phrases, rights,
which neglect these facts, are half-worthless.

" The essential nature is stirred by the essential life ;
by the real actual existence of love, and life, and character,
and by the real literature which takes in its spirit."

Bagehot was, therefore, a moralist, who judged politics,
as he criticized art, with a severe charity. What he asked
first in a British statesman was mental integrity. Palmerston, that " old man of the world " with his " frivolous
haughtiness " : Disraeli, separated by a gulf from " the
simple and earnest English nature " ; Canning, " the
changing talk of the practised talker running away about
all the universe " ; Gladstone, " undeniably defective in

the tenacity of first principle " ; Burke, who " saw a great truth and saw nothing else "—in all these Bagehot saw some defection from the steady, calm integrity of truth. A memorable eulogy of Pitt shows more of his ideal. " Uniformly Liberal " in the ground-plan of his ideas, he was the first modern Minister who applied his administrative gift to carrying through a scheme of thought ; he concludes that " in political instruction he was immeasurably superior to Fox, and that in the practical application of just principles to ordinary events he was equally superior to Burke."

The touch here on " ordinary events " is the secret of Bagehot's permanent hold upon us. Discerning, as few of his contemporaries did, the complexity of life, he had the supreme talent of seeing in it the simple things that mattered. To call him an amateur would be absurd, but he imparted professional knowledge with the amateur's true detachment. Complexity must be mastered ; " the speciality of pursuits is attended with a timidity of mind "; and his final comment on Macaulay's *History* was the disproportion of its length to events in themselves so insignificant.

His simplifying talent distrusted devices which, to him, masked and weakened the true aim, and he judged all such, from " ornate " poetry to proportional representation, with the same displeasure. Much of his teaching, therefore, consists in pointing the obvious truths which modern civilization tends to shroud, or to neglect. Thus, " the characteristic danger of great nations, like the Romans or the English, which have a long history of continuous creation, is that they may at last fail from not

comprehending the great institutions which they have
created." "The first duty of society is the preservation
of society." Forms of government are lightly made, but
"the life of a constitution is in the spirit and disposition
of whose who work it." The limits of free speech are
positive ; "no government is bound to permit a controversy which will annihilate itself." What Cromwell
called "providences," or in other words the teaching of
history, could not, Bagehot argued, be ignored, even by
those with the ten talents. "The characters which do
win in war are the characters which we should wish to
win in war." Property seemed to him still the most valid
of political tests ; "if it has been inherited, it guarantees
education ; if acquired, it guarantees ability."

There have been writers in whom such generalities
betray empty Prussianism, or superficial prejudice, but
with Bagehot the case is different. For he possessed the
precisely opposite power of deriving the complex from
the seemingly obvious—of tearing away the present veil
of convention. He set himself, then, to philosophize the
everyday things of life. He showed us the long agony of
man in the making, and bade us watch for the suppressed
savage who is ever breaking his prison bars. He taught
the difficulty of making a government at all, and our
facility in mistaking true opinion. The dry bones of the
constitution were clothed by him with life, the facts
severed from the fallacies, the grotesque from the
efficient.

Anthropology and history were brought to humanize
economics ; he transferred the custom, the competition,
the delicate web of character which he had diagnosed in

war and government, to capitalist industry and Lombard-street. And in all this he showed a rare appreciation of the work of Darwin and Huxley—the acceptance of growth, change, and variation, as the slow-moving laws of life. No wonder that he deprecated haste and asked for more meditation, for to the born intuitionist's wonder at the miracle of existence he added a knowledge of science, which cannot forget the tragedy of a hundred dead civilizations, or the forces that crush ignorant enthusiasms. " An inexperiencing mind," he called Macaulay's ; his own double experience from Nature was that change comes, but is always slow. " Other things being equal, yesterday's institutions are by far the best for to-day " ; his complete philosophy would have added, " but not for to-morrow."

Not the least potent quality in Bagehot's long literary life is a certain comforting insularity. We can all appreciate a writer who makes our stupidity a considerable political asset. Most men of British race hear with some satisfaction of the superiority of the amateur to the expert, of the " fresh " mind to the bureaucrat, of the British to the Latin, of the Cabinet to Congress. There is even an anti-clerical, sometimes an almost republican, chord which Bagehot struck, not without an echo of agreement. At least, his share of responsibility for the continuance of these consolations is considerable ; no writer is less cosmopolitan, and the inner deity of his constitutional shrine revealed himself, like Milton's, " first to his Englishmen."

Insularity being our most permanent possession, Bagehot's books, though not for that alone, have earned their length of days ; but the most famous, *The English Constitution*, being concerned with less lasting material than wealth or science, has suffered most from the half-century passed since publication, and will be the first, it is probable, to lose its hold. If read together with his earlier essays on "Parliamentary Reform" (part of which it incorporates), it must, in some large respects, be deemed out of date. The "deferential" England that encompassed Bagehot has vanished. Few members of the present Cabinet would probably agree that "the great political want of our day is a capitalist conservatism." An aggressive House of Commons does not keep Ministers from their beds, and the relations of Cabinet and legislature since 1872 have been almost inverted. Towards the Crown Bagehot held an unsympathetic tone and missed its future significance ; in part, perhaps, because, like most men of that age, he did not foresee Imperialism. Parliament's popularity and prestige are not nowadays so great, and public opinion is much more swayed by extra-parliamentary forces.

Yet, with all deductions, his book remains the best exposition of our working government available to the average citizen, and any who doubt the quality of the brick which Bagehot made marble should turn to the writings of Croker and the age of publicists just preceding, to the theory of Blackstone, or the mentality of Charles Greville. Others—Dicey, Anson, Redlich, Lowell— have since deepened much of Bagehot's work, but on certain crucial points the pioneer is still the most lucid guide. He demolished the "mixed," or Montesquieu, view of our constitution, and showed its unitary character.

He first theorized the *post*-Reform-bill practice of the House of Lords, and sketched the true functions of a modern revising chamber. He threw the first light on the central motive powers of our extraordinarily fused system—on the Prime Minister's office, on the Committee of the Whole, on the Cabinet's control of expenditure, on the relations of the two front benches ; on all, in fact, which truly explains how it is that the mother of Parliaments does her work so much better than her offspring.

One reiterated doctrine of Bagehot, not in this book only, is too far-reaching to be passed over, though it helps to explain the increasing irrelevance of this teaching to our own day. He was not a democrat and, boundless though his capacity was for spiritual expansion, his objections to democracy seem tolerably fundamental. Personal experience of Paris in 1851 had impressed him unfavourably with the " over-principled ruffians " who spouted " philosophical nonsense " over barricades, but the roots of his belief lay much deeper. The whole cast of his mind, his scientific studies, and practical experience alike led him to conclude that variation was the rule, and intelligence the salt, of life. " Every person," he wrote in 1859, " has a right to so much political power as he can exercise without impeding any other person who would more fitly exercise such power." The rule of mere numbers, or that of one caste, would each imperil that " system of removable inequalities " which his competitive brain commended, and would destroy that " supremacy of the central group of trained and educated men " which, on his view, must run a true Parliamentary government. Haste, excitement, ignorance, these were the old perils in the upward progress of man, which would be revived by the rule of the constituencies. The masterfulness of democracy appeared to him one of the plain teachings of history ; men would use in their own interest any wide and sudden concessions of the franchise.

But any inability to accept Bagehot's sweeping surveys as a whole does not in the least impair one's admiration for his method and fertility. They reappear, to assert the same principles, in *Physics and Politics*. All that Darwin and Maine were doing was here absorbed, applied to the life of nations, and brought down to the public discussion which the author took to be the best custodian of original energy. On the herd impulse, the imitative instinct, the tests of verifiable progress, whole libraries added since have done little more than elaborate Bagehot's single spies into battalions. It is in the last pages of this book that he rises, perhaps, to his greatest height of political predictive wisdom—leaving his sketch, of the struggle for national success, on that key of restrained optimism which belonged to his character.

His economic studies only transfer to another field his cherished articles of belief ; the " purging " force of nature, if left alone, the power of minorities to move mountains, the mighty influence of national habit, and the merit of palliatives as compared with revolutions. His peculiar faculty of elimination in dealing with tough material was as successful here as elsewhere. If on one side he taught us what political economy could not be asked to do, with the other hand he related it to physiology, to psychology, and to the everyday life of commerce.

Wholeheartedly he adopted the orthodox teaching of his master, Ricardo, which was deepened by his business training and his work on the *Economist*. He always liked the robuster virtues, and hated nothing so much as spoon-feeding, or the " soft and limp " mentality induced, as he thought, by over-legislation. He saw in big business the triumph of brain, predicted that the " monarchical " element in industry must increase, and frankly looked on the capitalist as a benefactor to society. But his chief aim was not to attempt new conclusions ; rather, to put political economy right with the public, to show that it was " not a questionable thing of unlimited extent, but a most certain and useful thing of limited extent." *Lombard Street* was a practical application, induced by Bagehot's special knowledge of banking. It has certainly initiated millions of untrained readers into the elements of our credit and currency fabric, the delicacy and dangers of which, so insisted on by Bagehot, received all the illustration most of us require from the period of the war. And here, too, with all the cards of critical knowledge on his table, he comes to a typically reasoned conservative conclusion.

The candid historian, or even those who find repellent the theory and practice of the Victorians, will judge Bagehot—not merely upon these works above-mentioned, but on the too neglected *Literary Studies* and *Biographical Studies*—to be the most searching and human interpreter of that age. Great in positive additions to knowledge, he was still greater for that attitude of mind which explains his permanent fame, filled with a clear and calm intellectual vitality that drew life from everything really living in man. No happy knack of style, nor even any perfectly trained art, will keep alive the political or economic conclusions of one generation ; nothing but humane and practical wisdom. From this is derived that prophetic gift which startles Bagehot's readers, a gift shared only by the greatest of political thinkers. The dark conservatism of Maine, the deepening pessimism of Lecky, cannot partake of the same long life.

Bagehot lives long because he was perfect compound of heart and head, because he could see reality without cynicism, and ideals without mistiness, or shadow of intolerance. Only the combination of a first-class brain, with a profound sympathetic knowledge of common life in England, could have done his work. And in one of his Somerset letters there is a saying which Shakespeare, the greatest man of his type, might have envied : " There is no time for quiet reflection like the intervals of the hunt."

CURZON

CURZON

THERE are two climacterics for the biographer : the first is that seized precisely by Boswell, the moment when knowledge is intimate but not final and the reader may yet kindle with memories of a living man ; the second, that taken by Monypenny or Masson, when in the fullness of time the hero can be detached from his valets, and when all the vital facts are known and, if known, can be revealed. And since the art strictly applicable to the one season is often transferred to the other, since impressionism tries to cut the essence of a great figure out of the whole canvas of the past, while on the other side pantechnicons or panopticons are laboriously manufactured for men just dead, of whom the truth cannot be known, four leading types of biography are always contesting the palm.

Judged by the canons of the art now dominant, Lord Ronaldshay's work falls into that " mixed " class which applies, to a man whom we have seen and known, the three tiers, the embracing monument, erected by research on any buried Cæsar. But the architecture of biography is, in truth, empirical ; if the house is good to live in and true to scale, that satisfies ; and on this, the most enduring test, the *Life of Curzon* will, its reader must feel, long withstand the searchings of time. The inner detail of Curzon's policy, or his relations with his colleagues, cannot in the nature of things be known for years to come; but meantime Lord Ronaldshay has succeeded—for most of us for the first time—in making alive that which was marble, and in giving a human and tangible Curzon to the generation to whom he gave himself, but to whom he never gave himself away. His figure becomes human because his biographer writes like a man, and we never hear the pen of the historian flagging, for the good reason that his subject is immersed in matter upon which his own labour has been lavished.

He deals with a life of sixty-six years, and to six of these he devotes more than a third of his space. Rightly, without a doubt ; for India made Curzon's fame, and by India he repeatedly asked to be judged. Yet as the qualities which went East, to make or mar, had their long embryonic stage, so even in the Indian volume, where the author has a larger room, he does well never to let us lose sight of Curzon's personality as his motif—strung up for India, stretched taut and snapped by India, the C major of his life. The book has high value as a political study of rare taste and judgment, but even more as a document of humanity will most men prize it ; and it is to the first volume, that shows this strong Victorian in germ, that they will, perhaps, more constantly return. One thing, in particular, most of us will wish to have known long before, that for the greater part of his life, and always in that rather grim anti-climax of it, Curzon was incessantly in pain. Raised against that background, his foibles become intelligible, his resolution admirable, and his life heroic.

It is in the third volume that the intrinsic defect of a " contemporary " biography first seriously affects us. The workmanship fully rises to the exacting demand of describing twenty crowded years ; the insight, pathos, and judgment are the same ; but what was felt occasionally in the Indian volume has become, with the story of the War Cabinet and the Peace Conferences, a patent, though an inevitable, drawback : the facts as a whole either are not available or, alternatively, cannot be told. And, together with this limitation imposed upon the biographer, a marked change in the subject and his setting makes a grey twilight of that formerly opulent sunshine. The Curzon who had vexed earth and heaven has now disappeared. Within his large, nervous physique, something seems to have snapped ; he makes decisions but only to recant them, and mystifies his followers as, plainly, he has more than once his biographer. It is, therefore, not surprising if sometimes this volume falters in its stride ; for on half a dozen matters of acute controversy—the Parliament Act, Women's Suffrage, the Irish settlement, the Montagu-Chelmsford reforms— Lord Ronaldshay is unable wholeheartedly to defend Curzon's course, or to tell the whole story. If the curtain could have been raised a little more upon these crises, we could have gladly bartered some of the excellently sensible pages on the war situation of Italy, or on the task of the Shipping Control Board.

Yet it is the highest tribute to his art that in reading of Curzon, thus fixed in the Lloyd-Georgian era, the pathos of human things strikes us hardest—becomes, indeed, now and then almost unendurable. Images of pity, a thing not predictable of this subject, pass the shutter of the mind—a pity for all things antique fallen upon new times. It is the Armada galleon firing vain broadsides over the top of the light craft attacking : the bull half blinded by darts, charging barriers in a new arena, with heart still pumping courage but depending on an obsolete ringcraft : it is almost another Agonistes, with vision extinguished, inwardly revolving the days of his strength. We learn here that the last great blow to Curzon's hopes, his rejection as Prime Minister in 1923, was officially put to him on the ground that, with a Labour Opposition concentrated in the House of Commons, it was impossible for the head of the Government to sit in the Lords ; and we are told with what magnanimity to the outer world, which is after all what matters, he swallowed the hemlock. But, if we read carefully his history from 1909 onwards, it is probable that we shall agree with a note of his own, made in a moment of depression, that he was " unfitted " to be Prime Minister. The something mysterious found by his biographer in his attitude to the Indian Reforms loses its mystery by repetition. He instigated opposition to Women's Suffrage and the Parliament Act, but in each case stage-managed a final retreat ; as with India, so in the latter stages of the Irish question, he seems to shy from a decision which he presumably detested, but a decision for which he must share the responsibility ; so, during 1921-22, he swallowed a policy in Egypt and the Near East which he continuously reprobated and later did much to reverse.

He protests, he memorializes, he abdicates, but he does not resign ; now, as thirty years before in India, he takes the rebuff—are there not work to be done, men to be kept out, evil to be borne that good may come ? We do not know whether the worn-out body was at last revenged upon the mind, or if the mental texture was itself working out a cumulative malady. But a constitutional leader must more than negatively accept his burden ; he does not live only *in foro conscientiæ* ; compromise must be his decision. It is legitimate to think that Curzon, whether through original character or through the wear of forty years' toil and suffering, was not in 1923 the Prime Minister suited to the needs of the hour, and that his disappointment may, for his ultimate fame, have been a blessing in disguise.

However this question be answered, it does not minimize his public services during the years of trouble from 1916 to 1923. We are still too near to apportion the praise due to the English ministers who restored peace in Europe and sincerity to Britain ; but it is impossible to read these pages without an increasing conviction of Curzon's rare patriotism and an increasing admiration for the toil which, not least in a sort of victory over his own character, made him one instrument in recovering for our country something like a moral contentment. This Hildebrand to himself and others claimed—and as we now recognize, with justice—that he had loved righteousness and hated iniquity, and like that much greater man died, in a very real sense, an exile.

With some persons unfamiliar, we must suspect, with Asia it has been the custom to call Curzon a man of words.

If true, it is a heavy condemnation of our age ; to be twelve years in the Commons (five of them in office), six years Viceroy, eight years leader of the Lords, a member of the War Cabinet, and Foreign Secretary, to rise so high in the period from 1886 to 1925, when Asia was reborn and Europe nearly perished, took a good deal more than words. In fact, whether we approve it or not, his Indian administration alone was one of enormous and lasting achievement. He created the Frontier Province, the Department of Commerce and Industry, the co-operative credit societies, the Railway Board and the Imperial Cadet Corps : he reorganized education from top to bottom, reformed the Secretariat and the Police, restored to India her national pride by protecting her monuments, opened contact with Tibet, founded agricul-tural research, launched modern famine relief, and de-vised new financial settlements with the Provinces ; to say no more. Modern India is his creation ; and it is small wonder that, go where we will, Curzon Sahib is the name of the restorer or maker that always strikes the ear. And when he fell from this apex, when his happiness, health, and policies seemed to suffer a universal shipwreck, the side-products of his industry would fill many average lives. The University of Oxford, another of the ancient causes which Curzon refused to look on as lost, was by him, as Chancellor, pushed and reasoned into the first instalments of modern change. His own solutions—a working men's college, for instance—were not always felicitous; his energy was not always rewarded ; but he at least got done what others had long deliberated. The

Royal Geographical Society, the National Gallery, the Everest expedition, Clive's statue, his work for national monuments at Tattershall, Bodiam or Walmer, the Lord Rectorship at Glasgow—it is always work, not always happily or with the gift of pleasing, but it is work, prepared for by industry, written, copied, and stamped with his own hand, sealed, signed and delivered.

If upon thinking of his life as a whole a sense of failure deadens the spheres vibrant with his activity, it is not, we think, because he was defeated in many of the public questions which he had most at heart. His controversy with the military and Lord Kitchener, the undoing of the partition of Bengal, the move of the capital, " in an evil hour " as he thought, to Delhi—on such matters he strove honourably, and may yet find defenders or vindication. Nor is popularity the decent test, or the frequent reward, of political greatness. " No statesman of such eminence," says the wise historian of Wolsey, " ever died less lamented " ; but the lack of public affection for Curzon is not the tragedy here. For time has avenged Castlereagh upon those who hooted his coffin. It is rather that he was one of the *ancien régime* who unwittingly make change inevitable ; who so hew and break the ground, that crops they have not sown spring up in the clean soil.

There is one characteristic of Lord Ronaldshay's book which holds, it may be, a clue to this warped achievement and to those endless Sisyphean labours. Curzon's colleagues in India are barely mentioned ; we hear nothing, for example, of the share of Thomas Raleigh in his legislative and educational reform.   If this to some extent robs the picture of completion, it is yet true in art. Curzon, one must conclude, lived and worked alone. One-man rule was his ideal from first to last ; alike in England, where he deplored the decadence of the Prime Minister's office since the all-seeing autocracy of Peel, and in India, where he would have abolished the Presidencies, and where he did in fact load the centralized burden of the Viceroy with superfluous work which no successor could carry.   That flowing and legible hand, disdaining labour-saving invention, was never at rest, and may be seen on the Simla files, in exhaustive peremptory criticism, descending to the cut of saddlery and the engagement of cooks.   Sir Walter Lawrence has told how his chief could not stop work, yet never found it satisfying ; and he certainly worked at the price of the nervous judgment, whose price is above rubies, and drowned decision in a stream of fact. His most fugitive essays, if we can use any epithet so fleeting, give a like impression ;   statistics master his moral, greatness is counted and not weighed.   " Efficiency of administration," he said, " is in my view a synonym for the contentment of the governed " ; hence, surely, the flaw in his ideal of labour, the venerable and encroaching delusion of devoted administrators.   High his standard was, even religious, but fixed with too little reference to human frailty and to professional pride, and insisted on as too obvious a truth.   His Convocation speeches at Calcutta, his addresses at many State Durbars, his administrative method—here were slashes of the rasping weapon used for a good end, which leaves the red scar behind. For though Curzon, to our thinking, lived alone, he loved his fellowmen, and would make them work with him by reference to their hearts or their reason; but by " taking the people into his confidence " he only meant that they should hear his views expounded before they were translated into action. It was thus by stimulus, as it were in a prolonged Durbar, by provocation, by reproach, that he made India move and think, and so prepared the end of the India which he wished to perpetuate. To create opinion is next to forcing it into the open, and the platform has no more certain exit than the polling booth.

If, finally, we attempt to appraise the powers and mentality of this remarkable man, we can hardly fail to be struck with the precocity of his youth and the ungrowingness of his mind. " Boyishness," we are told again and again of his humour ; boyish he certainly showed it to be with the Amir ; and every essential trait of the Viceroy was proved years before at the Union, and is stamped on the records of the Canning Club. In short, the flower nurtured by Oscar Browning and Jowett flowered early and struck no deep roots. His mind, drawing power from his devouring vitality, was exalted rather than imaginative, lofty rather than broad, encyclopædic rather than piercing. Ceaselessly ardent in pursuing knowledge, he won her less by power of thought than by act of storm ; he liked his horizons hard and firm, and his verities documented. We see him, watch in hand, as he swings in the net ascending to the monastery on Mount Athos, or as the stone hurtles down the precipice ; everything is noted, enumerated and applied, whether Babu adjectives, the history of the Kowtow, the surname of "the Private of the Buffs," or the minor epic of Napoleon's billiard table. The hand that uprooted apathy must tear also the drapings off mystery, and he who redeemed the Residency from squalor must explain away the Singing Sands.

Macaulay's mental confidence was warmed by the stream of his manly, kindliest, nature : Wolsey's pomp and circumstance were mixed with human clay : but about Curzon's work and writing there is a stress which makes it, if in one sense higher, less sane and enduring. Megalomania, or the wish to excel others, would be partial charges, and unjust ; for he did not merely see himself in the mirror that he pressed upon nature. Nor is the cheap reproach of " aristocracy " to the point ; he was too deeply read in the lore of power not to know where it was contained, and did he not lead the revolt of the elder sons against their relegation to the Lords ? There was, rather, in him a species of conservative Calvinism—a sense of the ordained fate and duty laid upon great peoples and ruling classes to inherit the earth. The Almighty, he told the Indian Civil Service, had set their hand upon " the greatest of His ploughs." With what spontaneity the words " corps d'élite " fell from him when he spoke of the English in India ! With what unconscious condescension he impressed, perhaps upon a Chief descended from the Sun, the privilege of a Viceregal visit ! Pitying from his heart the peasant at the well and the plough, for whom he worked in the night watches, he had neither patience nor understanding for the adolescent nationalism of the educated classes, as he had little with Germans or Russians who encroached on our predestined and justified monopoly of Asia. That England should rule India, was it not written on the rock ? that men should rule women, was it not graved in immutable law ? Hence, we think, came his profound misjudgment, expressed even in his most moving speech of farewell, of India, " so defenceless, so forlorn " : and hence the mistake, twenty years later, of rejecting the Indian aspiration for further political advance. Perceiving, or thinking he perceived, that the Indian martial classes, who had made the contribution of man-power to the War, were not interested, he argued thence that the Indian war effort was irrelevant to her political claims. Than which nothing could be more misleading ; for, apart from the fact that India was asked to pay £100,000,000 to the expenses of the War, the machinery of recruiting was in the latter stages mainly moved by enlisting civilian good will. So far as the War was India's, it had become one of India as a whole, and the fixed martial categories of Curzon's Durbar, of the Sikhs and Sir Partab Singh, had long disappeared.

So it was that, just as in his best pen-pictures of travel we feel " this is magnificent but not nature," he brought to the facts the interpretation which his mentality had exacted. The shade of what had been so majestical, of creeds and institutions once preponderant and glorious, roused in him an instant sympathy. He would clothe their shadow with substance and restore their mausoleums to stand sentinels of reminder. Kedleston and Government House, Humayun's tomb and Montacute, Fathpur Sikri and the Taj—these he would save from the lion and the lizard, and perpetuate for Englishmen to come what England had sprung from, seen, and conquered. To England he left Bodiam, that perfect shell of a native ruling caste; for himself he prepared the tomb in marble, which should commemorate a love like the mighty ones of old and the new honours won for an ancient name. Kedleston, Eton, Oxford, the Indian Civil Service—to these and other great hierarchies, much in the spirit of his favourite Gibbon, he had dedicated his labour. And though it must be the function of a higher statesmanship than his to blend and transcend these ranks and degrees into affections wider and more embracing, let it be said that they do exist, and that the public service of this Empire cannot do without them. If they have the glory of going on, they will recognize their benefactor, with all his faults ; and Curzon will hold the place that Curzon held.

He belonged to an age which has disappeared in a bloodless revolution ; and lived into one of those periods in which old landmarks slip past by the telegraph poles, and what is middle-aged seems prehistoric. If he had failings all his own, they were afflictions rather than moral flaws ; and in compensation he lived in an armoury of endowments and ideals. If pride of race, if love of country, if worship of beauty and power, if glory in action, are still to be held possessions of great price, Curzon will live long in the English mind as one who held these things up to idolatry.   The penalty that such a worshipper may be, and perhaps should be, asked to pay, in his own person he paid to the uttermost farthing : and the cosmos in which he projected his too much deliberated ego was a perpetual and an adorned image of his country.   Over his grave we may recall the answer given by the last Saxon King to the question how much of England he would surrender to Harold Hardrada—" seven foot's room, or so much more as he may need, seeing that he is taller than other men."

MONYPENNY AND BUCKLE'S "DISRAELI"

MONYPENNY AND BUCKLE'S
"DISRAELI"

ONLY nations with short memories can dispense with long books. We who have lived long have a right to the full history of our great men, to the documents which convey events as they, and not as later impressionists, have seen them. For that matter the full story has once to be told for the impressionist to exist at all ; and in this particular case, Monypenny and Buckle, to treat them familiarly as a classic, are the quarry from which later artists have drawn their material. Their volumes hold not only Disraeli's life but the whole epoch of party which he, above all men, created, and are certainly none too long for his party to re-read, now that that epoch at last is closed.

For we hear less now of the primroses round Hughenden, and since the last Earl of Beaconsfield's day strange Jeroboams have arisen who have made Israel to sin ; the moment seems fit to ask what this curious genius meant by Toryism, what was the virtue of the creed he professed, what new twist he imparted to a growth of two hundred years, and whether it can reach another age. Three times at least, in 1714, 1832, and 1906, men have stamped down the earth on its coffin ; and three times, wraith, impostor, or reincarnation, it has reappeared.

It has committed itself to the hands of the Anglicans Clarendon and Salisbury, of the Puritan Harley, the sceptic Bolingbroke, the Evangelical Liverpool, and the Jew ; it was Little England and low tariff under Queen Anne, Imperialist and "fair trade" with Victoria ; it stood still with Burke, and marched unwillingly with Canning ; glorified the State with Strafford and again with Chamberlain ; accepted *laisser faire* with Pitt and Peel. What, we may well ask, makes the unity of a body of doctrine which has attracted the genius of Hooker and Falkland, Wordsworth and Newman, and absorbed the radicalism of three ages in Bolingbroke, Disraeli, and Randolph Churchill ? Its high priests, its poets, renegades and critics, have given it different names and admired it for different reasons. Toryism, which Salisbury found bound up with "the honour of the country"—by which Churchill meant "the party of broad ideas and of a truly liberal policy"—which Bagehot defined as "enjoyment" and Newman as "loyalty to persons," strange word, in origin so ignoble, in its history containing such debasement, yet comprehending so much life, magnificence, and everlastingness ! Does any thread exist to lead us through the maze ?

The early sequences through which the Tories have passed are truly described, if we discount some little fantasy, in Disraeli's novels. The Church interest in which they first took shape came into existence to resist attack both from Rome and from Geneva, against whom was framed a defensive philosophy of Divine right and passive obedience. This always-precarious basis the folly of the last Stuarts broke into atoms ; and the Tory party of the

Augustans was new-composed of two factions, the relics of the Cavaliers and the old Whigs encouraged by Harley, Swift, and St. John in detestation of the militarism, the corrupt executive, and the moneyed supporters of William III. Before the union of these two groups could be completed, a last blow fell upon them from the Stuarts' armoury of error; innocent or guilty, they received to a man the stigma of Jacobite, and as a ruling party vanished till the accession of George III. In the fractional groupings and " interests," from which that self-styled " old Whig " recruited a corps to overthrow the Whig dynasties, again we discern two very different elements : on one side the janissaries, the ex-Jacobites, and the Jenkinsons ; but also, and more vital, that body of liberal or national Whigdom which descended from Bolingbroke and Carteret to Shelburne and the Pitts. The objects of George III, which he strove in vain to accomplish through twenty years of intrigue and humiliation, were turned to ends of which he had hardly shown himself worthy through the folly of Charles James Fox in the Coalition, and the act of God in the French Revolution. In this ordeal of fire and water the younger Pitt won to his side a third body, the Burke or anti-Revolution Whigs, and blended all three into the Tories whose exertions persisted through twenty-three years of war, and their enervation for another fifteen of peace. Intoxicated with Burke's rhetoric, so charged for these overdriven and average men with a fatal negation, the party whom Pitt had re-energized sank into a passive aristocracy, confused administrative competence with the art of statesmanship, stopped their ears to Canning, and were finally led by the deaf Wellington into the defile of 1832. From that the gifted Peel led them forth, not so much now a party as a perpetual rearguard, who shambled from one " untoward incident " to another, and saved their lives only by throwing away their arms. Once again Providence sent them a Messiah, in a form even less genial to them than the Whig Pitt or the dissenter Harley : a Messiah of strange race, loaded with watchchains, a dandy, an adventurer, a debtor. Disraeli spurred them from this rank parching wilderness of Conservatism, feeding them with strange new food he declared to be drawn from their treasures of old, and led them within sight of the high ground on which sparkled more than the minarets of his fancy— nothing less than the principles of Strafford and the practice of Pitt.

But he was old when they reached the Land of Promise, and died before the tribes were renumbered. Again they fell back on drums and trumpets of class blindness ; and while, as in a laboratory with double doors, Salisbury distilled honour and glory and peace for England, " the goats " in Victorian country houses were disporting themselves with Tory democracy. A third Sibyl spoke : Chamberlain tore himself from Gladstonianism, and came over with the Liberal Unionists to save the seed which Randolph Churchill had planted; and a third fusion of Whig and Tory ruled this Empire, with hardly a break, to 1906. These twenty years coincided with enormous armaments in Europe, war and gold in Africa, and a mental sirocco in the Orient, through all of which Salisbury, his new allies, and the disciples of his old age, carried England in safety and, as most men hold, in honour. But as this era came to an end, the legacy of Gladstone and Disraeli, a newly educated, enfranchised, and unsatisfied democracy, asked a strait account of their honourable economy ; and a storm arose in which all their makeshift moorings, Church schools or the Irish Union, strained and broke away. For the second time in a century the tragedy of a whole new world came to redress the Tories' shortcomings in the old ; the War of 1914 opened to them a broad unquestioned road of duty, and so remade the national fabric, plunged in such an aftermath of danger all the national institutions, that the Tories were enabled to make a long contribution towards the restoration of England; to do something to make her sane and secure, as the dead had known her, before they faced the aspirations of the dead men's children. That contribution, such as it was, is done, and will be for future history to appraise ; one can at least say that since 1919 the nation has psychologically moved much more than a decade, and breathes now what Clarendon once in like case called " its old good manners, its old good humour, and its old good nature." To the man who did this, posterity will not be ungrateful.

If this sketch be true of Tory history in the past, certain morals follow which bear upon its future. We deal, in the first place, with a party of the Right, clinging with tenacity to what their fathers have told them, and subject to all the ills that age is heir to. Inevitably it is apt to drag the chain of lost loyalties, superannuated leaders, and indefensible chivalries. Its doctrine is often clouded with polytheism and passing cults of the frontiers —Dr. Sacheverell and Flora Macdonald, non-jurors and *émigrés*, Governor Eyre and General Dyer. Taken in bulk, the Right have a horror of ideas, for is not the practical man, in Disraeli's words, " one who practises the blunders of his predecessors " ? For long tracts of their history they have indiscriminately resisted improvement, and in claiming to reverence their ancestors often reduce opinion to aged individual prejudice. Their position becomes safer, but more complex, when we add that this Right wing is incessantly overtaking the Left ; that it lives by repeated inoculation of Liberal ideas, and thus suffers from a never-perfected state of compromise. More than once, as we have seen, it has been shattered at a crisis because its last recruits were insufficiently absorbed ; and now and then happens a worse thing, when some new-comer of individual genius warps with his strong teaching the party's natural development. Pitt died in conflict with more than one mountain, for Pelion and Ossa were piled on him by the Conservative Burke.

And as those who defend the present are in fact claiming a right to interpret the past, the Tory party is nothing if not historically minded. From specific historical, or unhistorical, claims it sprang, and only in history can be found its philosophical defence. Its own version has sometimes been fanciful, but invariably insular ; and if, proceeding farther, we called it an English party, in distinction to Britain at large, historically we should not be much amiss. Though often thrown into opposition by the intrusion of some non-English energy—a Dutch King, a Hanoverian *camarilla*, or cosmopolitan finance—normally the old Tories boasted, and even yet are not wholly parted from, a relation of peculiar closeness to

Church and Crown, in whose cause their first founders threw themselves away in forlorn hopes and village sieges. From such history the Augustan Tories drew one maxim of perennial consolation : that on their side fought the permanent things of England, and that Toryism, left to itself and clear of foreign contagion, was agreable to nature. " How much time, how many lucky incidents, how many strains of power, how much money," Bolingbroke argued, was needed to make a Whig majority, while Toryism rose " by its natural genuine strength." If read as a reproach, his theory has still a valid meaning ; for, endowed as it is with the bent of a naturally conservative people, what follies, what timidity, what blindness must be present, if Conservatism in England is for long ejected from power.

The name of Bolingbroke, a man of the centre who turned to the fanatics of the far right to feed his ambition, exemplifies yet another conclusion from Tory history— that they, more perhaps than other parties, depend for their usefulness upon their leaders. " The placid contentment of the masses," to borrow Mr. Montagu's phrase regarding the old India he wished to awake, has been in normal times the attitude of the Tory to his leader ; if he has resisted, it has usually been when he thought the leader was going too fast, and he therefore refused toleration to Harley, Parliamentary reform to Pitt, the income-tax to Liverpool, and devolution to Wyndham. But any text-book will illustrate a pig-headedness that has some-times been fatal, and suggest that, if the leaders had waited upon their followers for policy, we should still be eating acorns. Yet this characteristic is the reverse side of what is their most fundamental virtue. If as a "country party" they began, and sometimes sank to a bucolic faction, their greatest minds rose to a vision of a nation organic in that it is made up of living cells, multiform in life, yet integral and corporate. "To love the subdivision, to be attached to the little platoon"; as Burke preferred to represent the living interests of natural inequalities rather than even, sawn, lengths of population, so he drew rules of public policy from the morals descended, as he held, from heaven to every hearth. What, asked Canning and Coleridge, is "the State"? Is it anything but the combination of countless real societies, smaller but more venerable, more lovely, nearer home? We have learned something, of late, of these rival allegiances, and know better than our fathers that, if the State is to remain supreme, it can be only in realizing its limitation, and by founding its unity not in uniformity, but in difference. And Toryism, which existed before Acts of Union, Enclosure Acts, or even the Prayer-book of 1662, is the last thing that need buttress its history on these generalizing measures, born of temporary emergency.

Generalization, indeed, is a fruit of the intellect, an attribute from which the Tory shrinks as from a guilty thing. Not improperly, if (as Lord Randolph used to say) "rightly understood," for no teaching of conservatism can rest, ultimately or in large degree, on an intellectual base. Individual reason, or a philosophy of material experience, abstract and metaphysical right, bare utility— on all these gaunt and pretentious redoubts Hooker, Newman, Burke, and Coleridge levelled their heaviest ordnance. To abjure wholesale dependence on a mental gift which all must use is a standing temptation to sloth, sentiment, and inanity ; but the Tory protest of anti-rationalism is real when it bids us mark an *aliquid divinum* in government, a concreteness in history, and a prerogative in time. For man, even economic man, is a noble animal, but the conscience he does not tend burns like a flame ; life, brief candle, is lighted at fires not of our making ; there are things auguster than the majority of our contemporaries, more comprehending than the largest individual brain, a treasury of merit hoarded in the past, and a reality in prosaic fact which theory may condemn but is powerless to destroy. Toryism is thus dogmatic, and claims its dogma as *ex cathedra* : infallible, not as voicing one party or one age, but as the deposit of a long life, a tested revelation, a living society.

These are high claims ; and one is conscious of their absurdity if measured only by those gentlemen who, like Peel, " never see the end of a campaign " ; but they are the veritable teaching of the seminal minds in the Tory tradition. That tradition undergoes development, and is reinterpreted every few generations by the society built round it ; and sharp divergences of policy at different stages of party history demonstrate that the Tories, like others, cohere not in a programme but in a temper or a spirit. Only in the spirit of their whole tradition, our re-reading of this biography suggests, can they hopefully embark on the central difficulties of a new age. Attempts have been made, with the credentials of learning, to impugn the continuity of that tradition ; to argue that, Charles I and Queen Anne being so indubitably dead, the policies of Strafford and Swift walk not, neither should they talk, and that we should begin our history with the Reform Bills. Now, passing over the fact that principles do not die like kings and politicians, this criticism seems to miss the essence of the English political system ; which is, in brief, that as compared with other countries we have had no revolutions, that our Right has never been exclusively clerical or dynastic, our Left never wholly cosmopolitan and proletarian, that our divisions are fixed not in provincial or legitimist feuds, military autonomy or class hatred, but come in unbroken descent from a people of " removable inequalities," used for three centuries to public discussion. This in itself involves the easy succession and moderation of our political groups, and ensures the existence of a large, perhaps the largest, *bloc* in the middle, those notorious pendulum-swingers whose weight strikes the hour in tune with the earlier and sensitive note of their leaders. For leaders they have ; and the history of England is made, if we are candid, much less by the Shaftesburys and Walpoles, Salisburys and Harcourts, than by a Halifax or a Godolphin, the trimmers, Peelites, and mugwumps, who cannot help seeing both sides of a question, and commonly delay decision till all is saved, save honour. The number of children born alive who defy Gilbert's law is really very considerable ; and in a country where political arrangement is much older than economic regimentation, thousands will continue to surprise the best laid schemes of party organisers.

Our parties work, then, like the cotton trade, in an atmosphere of perpetual damp, and are ruled by a system much older than themselves ; and any sketch of party evolution is not, therefore, and fortunately, to tell the best work that a party has done. We do not claim exclusive credit for the Tories when we review Peel's sound police and finance, Disraeli's social legislation, the foreign policy of Salisbury, or the local government reform of Goschen and Chamberlain ; a trend, of course, is given by the party or its leaders, but the public conscience, educated opinion, or the voice of a prophet outside politics, determine the limits of action.

Such considerations, which give conservative opinion at least a parity of chances with its rival, must be offset by the appearance of others, new since Disraeli's day and threatening the very continuity to which allusion has been made. A new mobility of mind and body weakens the traditional bases of Tory power. Its old foster-mother, the Church of England, can hardly in the changed conditions be claimed as a supporter, and the fixed society of Miss Mitford and Trollope has almost disappeared. A cheap and "rationalized" Press, the erasing power of a uniform education, and ceaseless transport of men and ideas, have broken the old cadres of Toryism and thrown it, to sink or swim by its wits, into a competitive world. Most of all, a war like none ever fought before has enthroned a new ruler of democracy, of proved might but incalculable feeling, an unknown soldier.

Disraeli's party will, therefore, perhaps do well to realize that they are sitting in inquest on something more than a Central Office. The deceased, long domiciled among us, is the Whig era, *alias* the Reformation ; in no sense of the theologians, but as a connected mass of politico-economic achievement. We bury in one broad grave *laisser faire* and Acts of Union, congested sovereignty and unrestricted private property, strong men who kept the house armed but whose beneficence was exhausted. The generation coming on fight on a ground cleared of many antagonisms of Disraeli's youth. No one now would sell a colony, defend a class tariff, or even, perhaps, force the disendowment of a Church ; the contrast, on the other hand, between public and private property is shading away into fine differences of commissions, supervision, and control. But whether those who follow Disraeli have thought out, as he surely would, the full implications of political democracy, is neither time nor place to say ; whether they accept the logic of what they themselves have done in England and the Empire ; whether, for example, they admit that civic equality involves economic redistribution.

The resources, certainly, of the long history which Disraeli invoked are not exhausted. From its full background we can pick out the vigorous figures whom his brush revived, the men who accepted fact and fought on principle, and can frame for ourselves with some degree of certainty a concept of action. The wheel having come full circle in the circumscribed revolutions of our race, we deal, however superficially changed the outward phenomena, with the political elements obtaining when Whig and Tory first took their being. A powerful State enthroned over delegated sovereignties, a balance of classes, restricted capitalism, a mercantile policy—for the practical conduct of these things the next generation must look to itself ; but if they seek basic principles wherewith to oppose weak sentiment and suicidal economics, they can carry Disraeli's teaching back to its next logical term, and examine the statesmanship of Burleigh and Strafford.

A long book, but Salisbury told us to use large maps ; and a long book is good when there is " time to think." Time, that is, before the deluge ; for, as Falkland liked to say, " I pity unlearned gentlemen in a rainy day."